PENGUIN BOOKS

THE NATURE OF MASS POVERTY

John Kenneth Galbraith is Paul M. Warburg Professor of Economics, emeritus, of Harvard University. He was born in 1908 in Ontario, Canada. After graduating from university in Canada and taking a Ph.D. at the University of California, he taught first there and then at Harvard and Princeton. During the Second World War he was in charge of wartime price control, for which he received the Medal of Freedom and the President's Certificate of Merit. Later he was a director of both the US Strategic Bombing Survey and the Office of Economic Security Policy in the Department of State. He has been closely identified with the Democratic Party and from 1961 to 1963 was American Ambassador to India. Recently he became an Honorary Fellow of Trinity College, Cambridge. He is a member for literature and a recent past President of the American Academy of Arts and Letters.

Professor Galbraith's books, many of which are published by Penguin, include *American Capitalism*; *The Great Crash 1929*; *The Affluent Society*; *The Liberal Hour*; *The Non-potable Scotch*; *The New Industrial State*; *Ambassador's Journal*; *Economics, Peace and Laughter*; *Economics and the Public Purpose*; *Money: Whence It Came, Where It Went*; *The Age of Uncertainty*; *The Nature of Mass Poverty*; *The Anatomy of Power*; *A View from the Stands*; *Capitalism, Communism and Coexistence* (with Stanislav Menshikov); *A History of Economics*; and, most recently, *The Culture of Contentment*. He is also the author of a book of satirical sketches, two bestselling novels and a study of Indian painting (with M. S. Randhawa). His volume of memoirs, *A Life in Our Times*, was published in 1981. He delivered the Reith Lectures in 1966.

Professor Galbraith is married with three sons and lives in Cambridge, Massachusetts.

JOHN KENNETH
GALBRAITH

The Nature of Mass Poverty

PENGUIN BOOKS

PENGUIN BOOKS

Published by the Penguin Group
Penguin Books Ltd, 27 Wrights Lane, London W8 5TZ, England
Penguin Books USA Inc., 375 Hudson Street, New York, New York 10014, USA
Penguin Books Australia Ltd, Ringwood, Victoria, Australia
Penguin Books Canada Ltd, 10 Alcorn Avenue, Toronto, Ontario, Canada M4V 3B2
Penguin Books (NZ) Ltd, 182–190 Wairau Road, Auckland 10, New Zealand

Penguin Books Ltd, Registered Offices: Harmondsworth, Middlesex, England

First published by Harvard University Press 1979
Published in Pelican Books 1980
Reprinted in Penguin Books 1993
1 3 5 7 9 10 8 6 4 2

Printed in England by Clays Ltd, St Ives plc
Set in Monotype Baslerville

Contents

Preface

This book had its origins almost two decades ago in India. In those years, the early sixties, the United States had a large and costly program of assistance to Indian agriculture. Its purpose was to help increase Indian food supplies and to lessen, however slightly, the poverty which is the fate of nearly all in India who make their living from the land. One did not doubt that our motives were humane as well as sensibly self-interested. But I soon became persuaded that our efforts were sadly misguided and that the error extended on to the Indians with whom we worked.

What we had decided were the causes of poverty with which the Indians and we sought to contend was derived not from thought but from convenience. There were, broadly speaking, only two things we could provide to lessen the deprivation – we could supply capital and, in principle, useful technical knowledge. The causes of poverty were then derived from these possibilities – poverty was seen to be the result of a shortage of capital, an absence of technical skills. The remedy included the diagnosis. Having vaccine, we identified smallpox. Only by accident could a therapy so selected be successful. There was, alas, no such accident.

My thoughts, accordingly, turned to a more valid explanation of mass poverty and the associated remedial response, so far as one can reasonably be offered, and I continued to reflect on this after my return to Harvard in 1963, where I resumed courses that I had previously initiated on the problem of development in the poor lands. But I had first to finish *The New Industrial State* and *Economics and the Public Purpose*, the large enterprise on which I was launched before going to India. And there were other diversions, including politics and the continuing and highly unrewarding distraction of the Vietnam war.

Finally, time and the opportunity came. In the winter of 1977, my colleagues at the Graduate Institute of International Studies of the University of Geneva encouraged me to schedule a series of lectures on the subject, and these I later revised and repeated at the Radcliffe Institute.

When publication of this book was discussed, Arthur Rosenthal, the director of the Harvard University Press, heard my reference to the lecture-room antecedents with grave alarm. It was the reaction of an experienced and discriminating man, the survivor of much pain. For it is the aberration of nearly all professors that they can publish their lectures, as it is the aberration of great business executives that they can make pamphlets of their speeches on the case for free enterprise. Subject matter apart, what is meant to be heard cannot be read. A lecture or speech is naturally discursive, for the audience needs time for digestion. For the average listener there must also be occasional repetition. When reading, he can, as he needs, go back over the material himself. So, as a broad rule, no lecture or speech should ever be published. And, if published, it should never be read. These chapters originally were lectures; they have been rewritten and now, I trust, are by way of being a book.

I begin with consideration of the seemingly sensible explanations we now regularly offer of the poverty of the poor country and the way these causes evaporate when tested against practical experience.

J.K.G.

Cambridge, Massachusetts

Acknowledgements

Andrea Williams, as ever on my behalf, made this manuscript decently publishable. Emeline Davis, Edith Tucker, and Anita Bers gave it much intelligent care. My colleagues Kenneth Arrow and Dwight Perkins read the manuscript and corrected me on numerous small points, urged useful further thought on matters that were by no means small. My warm, even affectionate, thanks to all.

I

How Poverty Is Now Explained

To be poor is believed by many who are, and most who are not, to be an unpleasant thing. If there is a difference of opinion here between the rich and the poor, it is in the depth of feeling on the subject, something on which practical experience will be thought to heighten sensitivity, although this is not wholly certain. There is a strong possibility that in many societies the poor react to their economic situation with less anxiety than do the rich, a point to which I will return.

Two forms of poverty can be distinguished. There is that which afflicts the few or, in any case, the minority in some societies. And there is the poverty that afflicts all but the few in other societies.

The causes of the first kind of poverty, that of the poor individual or family in the predominantly affluent community, have been much investigated and debated. What characteristics – moral, genetic, familial, environmental, educational, racial, social, hygienic – cause some persons to be excluded from the general wellbeing? This, the cause of case poverty, remains a question of considerable importance. Study has yet to produce general agreement. There remains even a residue of thought which holds that those who so suffer were divinely intended for their fate or have been accorded the suffering that, from personal deficiency, they righteously deserve. But this is not the kind of poverty with which I am here concerned.

My concern is with the causes of poverty in those communities, rural in practice, where almost everyone is poor – where, if there is wealth or affluence, it is the exceptional fortune of the few. The causes of this mass rural poverty, in contrast with case poverty, have been much less investigated. Instead, to an astonishing degree, the causes are simply assumed. When explanations are sought, numerous and exceptionally confident answers are given. When examined, these answers have one feature in common: they are universally unsatisfactory.[1] They are subject to contradiction by practical experience or they confuse cause with consequence or, while they serve casual conversational purpose, no one wishes to risk them in serious scientific discourse. Or, as noted in my preface, they are selected not for their validity but for their convenience.

The most common explanation of mass poverty, one which is offered at all levels of professional sophistication every day, is that the community, usually the country, is 'naturally poor'. This has reference to the

1. For a thoughtful and influential survey of such causes and the changing fashions therein, see Albert O. Hirschman, *The Strategy of Economic Development* (New Haven: Yale University Press, 1958). Professor Hirschman suggests that the explanations of poverty are so numerous that, if taken seriously, development is excluded. 'Their cumulative impact on the unwary reader could well raise serious doubts about the possibility of any economic development at all' (p. 2).

physical endowment: the soil is rocky, arid, or insufficient; there are few minerals, hydrocarbons, or other natural resources. When too many people struggle with this meager and recalcitrant environment, the result is inevitable: they divide a small return; all are poor.

Were Japan a poor country, its poverty would be explained along the lines just given. It is a mountainous cluster of offshore islands with little good soil, few minerals, no oil, but many people. Japan's catastrophic natural endowment goes unmentioned only because it is rich. Of Taiwan, were its people poor, the same would be said.

Since the Second World War, four hitherto poor communities have enjoyed a great and sustained increase in widely distributed income. They are regularly cited as models of successful development. One is Taiwan just mentioned; Singapore, Hong Kong, and Israel are the other three. (Many would now add South Korea.) None is favored as to land or natural resources. Singapore and Hong Kong are uniquely devoid of both. On the other hand, Iran and the Arabian peninsula are all rich in the currently most cherished of resources, which is oil. The ordinary citizen of Iran and most of those of greater Arabia live brief lives in a squalor not appreciably improved over that of their forebears in the then-embracing empire of the Sassanids and Shapur I. In the United States, West Virginia, a state with a singularly rich store of natural resources – water power, forests, superb seams of coal – regularly ranks among the bottom five states in per capita income. Connecticut, with poor land, no natural resources beyond some long-exhausted iron mines and a few underprivileged forests, ranks first. The relation of resources to well-being is so erratic as to be flatly worthless.

The next most commonly offered explanation of poverty and well-being invokes the nature of government and the economic system. A reference to resource endowment as a cause of poverty is made casually. The economic system as a cause of poverty is invariably cited with passion. The people are poor because they have not perceived the advantages of free enterprise, free competition and the market. Their energies, accordingly, are frustrated by a stupid and costly bureaucracy. Alternatively, they are poor because they are exploited; the surplus that they produce is appropriated by predatory landlords or capitalists. And this poverty persists because, since all goes to the owners of property anyway, there is no incentive to improve. Productivity remains stubbornly low. Since the period immediately following the Second World War when both, in effect, won independence, China under Communist auspices has almost certainly done far more to conquer mass poverty than has India, which, while it employs socialist rhetoric, remains a property-owning republic with capitalist entrepreneurs who, for studied rapacity, can probably claim to be the equal of any. But Hong Kong, Singapore, and Taiwan have all made greater progress than China. All are indubitably capitalist. This experience suggests that it makes far less difference as regards the causes or conquest of poverty whether a country is capitalist or Communist than whether it is Chinese or not. And the latter is an explanation that both socialists and non-socialists would join in rejecting.

Eastern Europe, at a somewhat higher level of well-being, shows the practical unwisdom of stressing the economic system as a cause of or an antidote for poverty. Let it be supposed that in 1880, the railroad by then being a thing of reasonable comfort and convenience, one journeyed around Eastern Europe over the territory that is now celebrated as the socialist camp. The highest and best-distributed standard of living would have been found in what is now the German Democratic Republic. The next highest would be in Bohemia, now in Czechoslovakia, followed by Slovenia and Croatia in what is now Yugoslavia. Hungary and the Austrian and German parts of Poland, Romania, and Bulgaria would be yet poorer. Poorer still would be Macedonia, Montenegro, and parts of Serbia. East, across the border in Imperial Russia, the living standards of Poles and Ukrainians would also be exceedingly mean.

Nearly a hundred years have now passed. For a third of this time these countries have been Communist. The same journey today (which might, on occasion, employ the same railway carriages) would show virtually the same *relative* states of prosperity and poverty. The East Germans remain, by a substantial margin, the most affluent (recent calculations suggest that per capita income in the GDR now approaches or maybe exceeds that of Britain) followed by the Czechs and the Slovenes. Macedonians, Montenegrans, and many Serbs are still very poor. The others would be in between.

And not only does the ranking remain generally unchanged as between countries, it remains undisturbed within countries. Yugoslavia, in this connection, is worth a special glance. In 1880, Slovenia and Croatia, now the northern states of the republic, had, as noted, a relatively high standard of living. Macedonia, Montenegro, and the Kosovo region of Serbia were wretchedly poor. The same general relationship persists. Between 1948 and 1972, total domestic production in Slovenia, the richest area of Yugoslavia, increased at an average annual rate of 6·9 per cent. In Kosovo, the poorest region, the growth rate averaged 6·1 per cent. However, the rate of population increase was three times as high in Kosovo as in Slovenia – from 1950 to 1971, 22·8 per thousand as compared with 7·5. In consequence, the per capita product of Slovenia, which was three times that of Kosovo in 1947, was 5·7 times that of Kosovo in 1972. The *difference* in per capita income between Slovenia and Macedonia, Montenegro, and Bosnia-Herzegovina also increased in these years, although less sharply.[2]

Slovenia and Croatia, the two relatively prosperous parts of Yugoslavia, were, like Czechoslovakia, Hun-

---

2. 'Yugoslavia's Socio-Economic Development, 1947–1972', *Yugoslav Survey* XV, no. 1 (February 1974): pp. 33–4. Yugoslav planning promises 'a faster development of all economically underdeveloped republics, and the fastest development of the Socialist Autonomous Province of Kosovo . . . aimed at *lessening relative differences* in the level of their development'. *Social Plan of Yugoslavia*, 1976–80, p. 74. (Italics mine.) This one takes to mean that it is now accepted that the differences in living standards are too stubbornly ingrained soon to be overcome.

gary, and the more prosperous parts of Poland, ruled from Vienna before the First World War. For assessing the causes of poverty in Eastern Europe, it is obviously more important to ascertain whether the country or region in question belonged before 1914 to the Austro-Hungarian (or German) Empire than to assess the modern impact of Communism.

I've so far been concerned with the comparatively persuasive explanations of poverty. Another set of causes, which, in fact, could be consequences, are more self-evidently simple-minded. Thus it is regularly said that the country is poor because it lacks capital for development. It is fully as informative to say that it lacks capital for development because it is poor. Savings for investment accrue only when there is a surplus beyond what is required for immediate consumption. Where poverty is general, there is no such surplus.

Similarly, it is said that the country is poor because it lacks trained, educated, or experienced technical and administrative talent. Few ever emerge to comment on the poverty of the new African countries without some such observation. Educated manpower is likely to be scarce in a country that has been unable, because of its poverty, to afford an educational system. Industry also is an aspect of affluence – of a standard of living that goes beyond food, elementary clothing, and elementary shelter that come from the land. If, being poor, the country has no industry, it will be devoid of people trained and experienced in the management of industrial enterprises. If the absence of trained and experienced people is a cause of poverty, it is as surely a result.

Cause and consequence are equally interchangeable in the common assertion that poverty is the result of ineffective, erratic, corrupt, or otherwise inadequate government. Economic development, it is said, is stifled by the exactions or inconsistent regulations of corrupt, foolish, or unpredictable officials. Necessary reforms – the abolition of backward and predatory landlordism – become impossible. So does effective encouragement of private enterprise or the efficient management of public enterprise. But poverty is surely a cause of under-financed and otherwise inadequate public administration. Also, where private sources of income are meager, public predation becomes attractive. Only a well-financed government, enrolling well-qualified people, is able to advance its policies and impose its discipline, negative or affirmative, in consistent and continuing fashion. So the quality and character of government is a function of the income of the people by which it is supported. Poverty is both a cause and a consequence of what Gunnar Myrdal has called the soft state.[3]

This last point is of much political importance, for on no matter has the effect of uninformed action been more distressing. Advice on economic development in the last thirty years has come extensively from economists and technicians of the rich countries. They have seen what has worked well in these lands and, not surpris-

3. Gunnar Myrdal, *Asian Drama: An Inquiry Into the Poverty of Nations* (New York: The Twentieth Century Fund, 1968). This is also available in abridged form in an edition published by Pantheon (New York: Pantheon, 1971), and future citations in this volume will be to that edition.

ingly, have advised the same for the poor countries. Planned public and private investment, education, agricultural extension, public works, public development of industry, have been so urged. And all too often these have foundered on the administrative or political inadequacy derived from the poverty they were meant to cure.

That the politics of poverty is different from the politics of affluence has also been hard for politicians of the affluent countries to perceive. People of affluence and associated capacity for expression have recourse against the state – they can be heard in condemnation of political behavior of which they disapprove, and they have the sanction of sacking the offender. Their politicians and officials respond in their behavior, act with a caution, decorum, attention to individual rights, that come to be assumed. The poor in the poor country have no similar capacity for assertion. Poverty makes the task of daily survival far more compelling. Illiteracy is also a rather obvious bar to self-expression. These factors, in combination with a far smaller pool of talent from which politicians are chosen, mean a far less rigorous standard of political performance. In recent years in the United States and elsewhere, much point has been made of the erratic and, on occasion, exotic behavior in the United Nations of certain of the Third World countries. Part of this criticism has been of the lack of docility in accepting the leadership or, at a minimum, the guidance of the rich countries. But some has been of behavior which is integrally a part of the politics of poverty. That different standards should apply to rich countries and poor, that sympathy and toleration are more appropriate than condescending hostility, should have been far more evident to some of our past representatives in the United Nations than in practice it was.

Next among the causes of poverty are the greatly mentioned unmentionables. One of these is intrinsic ethnic tendency. Englishmen are, or used to be, more industrious than the Irish, the Germans more so than the French or the Poles, the Swiss than the Italians, the Chinese and the Japanese than anyone else. No one within memory has explained in conversation the relative prosperity of the Indian Punjab, the squalor of Calcutta, and the perpetually perilous conditions of life in Bangladesh without reference to the diligence, high mechanical aptitude, and general progressiveness of the Punjabis, the amiable, articulate anarchy of the Bengalis.

It is the singular feature of such ethnic explanation that it is all but exclusively confined to conversation. The reputable scholar unhesitantly adverts to it in casual interchange, rarely if ever puts it in his books or even his lectures. What is wholly plausible in conversation is wholly impermissible in print. There is obviously something odd about an explanation of poverty and well-being that must be so discreetly handled.

Climate or latitude as a cause of poverty is treated with somewhat similar ambiguity. The circumstances here are not subject seriously to question. The tropics the world around are regions of very low income. Likewise, if less clearly, the sub-tropics. General affluence is exceptional, and the exceptions are countries such as Colombia and Kenya where altitude counters latitude to produce a moderate climate. In the temperate zone affluence is far more nearly the rule. And within the larger affluent nations there is a recognizable tendency for incomes to decline as one moves from north to south, or in the southern hemisphere from south to north. Conversational reference to the lower incomes of the southern American states, southern Spain, southern Italy, southern India, or northern Brazil has long been commonplace.

This explanation of poverty or well-being has by no means escaped scholarly notice. Ellsworth Huntington, the noted Yale geographer of the early decades of this century, in *Civilization and Climate*, and S. F. Markham in his much slighter *Climate and the Energy of Nations*, both associated the moderately cool areas of the globe, which are also subject to change in weather and season, with greater mental and physical activity and initiative.[4] The tropics, in contrast, involve an easier life and greater consequent lassitude, and their populations are more subject to endemic disease. Huntington concluded that climate 'first . . . has a direct effect upon man's health and activity. Second, it has a strong indirect but immediate effect through food and other resources, through parasites, and through mode of life. Third . . . it has been a strong factor – some would say, the strongest – in causing migration, racial mixture, and natural selection.'[5] Markham narrowed the effect of climate down

4. Ellsworth Huntington, *Civilization and Climate* (New Haven: Yale University Press, 1924); S. F. Markham, *Climate and the Energy of Nations* (London: Oxford University Press, 1942).

5. Huntington, p. 3. Huntington also had views on the relation of race to civilization which would enhance the task of a Yale president if offered currently by one of his professors. 'Initiative, inven-

largely to temperature: 'The nation which has led the world, leads the world, and will lead the world, is that nation which lives in a climate, indoor and outdoor, nearest to the ideal.'[6] To such explanations of poverty, modern students of economic development have reacted with extreme caution. Detailed mention is rare in the standard works, although passing references ('the enervating effect of heat on Indian productivity is a factor that can hardly be under-estimated'[7]) do occur.

Explanations of poverty have most often been made by people in the rich countries of the poor. But a lesser current of explanation has run from the poor countries to the rich. Of these explanations the legacy of colonialism is the most important. Colonial rule deliberately enforced industrial backwardness for reasons of commercial interest, destroyed self-confidence, created habits of dependency. All this explains the present misfortune. What is not explained is why this effect was so

---

tiveness, versatility, and the power of leadership are the qualities which give flavor to the Teutonic race. Good humor, patience, loyalty, and the power [sic] of self-sacrifice give flavor to the negro' (p. 35). He did insist, however, that the fine qualities of the white races were quickly lost in the tropics. A missionary in Central America, 'a most austere man, a member of a small and extremely devout sect', told of this effect as follows: 'When I am in this country [the Central American republic], evil spirits seem to attack me ... When I am at home in the United States I feel pure and true, but when I come here, it seems as if lust were written in the very faces of the people' (p. 75).

6. Markham, op. cit., p. 24.

7. Stanley Wolpert, *A New History of India* (New York: Oxford University Press, 1977), p. 4.

diverse – highly adverse in some parts of Africa and Latin America but much less so in other parts of these continents. There is a question also as to how long this explanation can be made to serve. Latin America has now had a century and a half of independence. Is the legacy of colonialism still a force? There is also the problem as to how the English-speaking colonies of the British Empire emerged so successfully from this blight and why a centuries-old tradition of independence did little for Ethiopia and not much for Thailand.

A more sophisticated explanation from the Third World, that developed by Raúl Prebisch, holds that poor countries, producers in the main of raw materials and agricultural products, suffer persistently in the terms of their trade with the industrial lands. Agriculture and the materials industries produce more labor than they require – are labor-expelling. Manufacturing and like industry produce less labor than they require – are labor-absorbing. Accordingly, the poor countries, being producers of agricultural and primary products, have a persistent surplus of labor. Wages, and therewith prices, are kept down by this surplus of labor and the associated need to expel it to industry. Wages, costs, and prices in the rich, industrialized countries are kept up by the need to absorb labor – draw it from agriculture and other primary production.[8] To these circumstances one might add the effect of differences in market structure – between numerous, different, and weak agricultural procedures and the oligopolistic strength inherent

8. This is an abbreviated form of Dr Prebisch's thesis. For a detailed statement, see his *Towards a Dynamic Development Policy for Latin America* (New York: The United Nations, 1963), p. 78.

in the positions of General Motors, Shell, DuPont, Nestlé, and the other characteristically powerful oligopolists of the industrial countries.[9] This disparity in power explains and perpetuates the poverty of the poor countries – of the Third World.

There is merit in this general range of argument, as I will later suggest. The equilibrium of poverty is sustained by the people it generates. Any partial escape leads to the increase in population and labor supply that arrests further improvement. But no argument that holds, merely, that producers of elementary foods and raw materials are at a disadvantage, destined to be poor, can be sustained. The evidence again intervenes. As producers of primary products – wheat, corn, soybeans, cotton, coal, wood pulp – the United States and Canada are pre-eminent. New Zealand and Australia are very important. It is these affluent countries that account for by far the largest share of the international trade in elementary food and like products. If to be a producer of primary products – a hewer of wood and a hauler of water for others – places a country in the Third World, then the United States, as I've often urged, is, by a wide margin, the first of the Third World nations.

The point has by now been made – perhaps to an extreme. Poverty is man's most powerful and massive affliction. It is the progenitor of much further pain – from hunger and disease on to civil conflict and war

9. This is a case I have made in *American Capitalism: The Concept of Countervailing Power*, rev. ed. (Boston: Houghton Mifflin, 1956), chap. IX.

itself. The past thirty years have been ones of singular peace in and between affluent countries. Very few people, a nearly infinitesimal number, have died in civil conflict within the rich countries of the non-Communist world. None at all have died in conflict between the rich countries of the non-Communist world or between these countries and those of the affluent socialist lands. In and between the poor countries conflict has been widespread and widely lethal, and it continues.

Yet of the poverty that induces to conflict, as we see, we have no explanation. Or, more precisely, we have a plethora of explanations, each superficially persuasive, each confidently offered, each notable for what it does not explain. In the commonplace explanations the exceptions regularly outflank the rule. Were malaria, smallpox, tuberculosis, or syphilis as variously diagnosed as poverty, one would not wish to risk being treated. We must see if we can find an explanation of poverty – more plausibly, a group of consistent explanations – that serves better than those now so casually advanced. But first we must look a little more closely at the factors, intellectual and social, which shaped our present assumptions as to causes.

2

The Political Origins of Error

Until the Second World War, there was relatively little serious discussion of the causes of mass poverty, and likewise very little of its remedy. As the colonial world had no claim to self-government, so it had no great claim to the consideration of its economic and social problems. Independence was a far more preoccupying goal than economic development. National leaders such as Mahatma Gandhi and Jawaharlal Nehru were largely content to assume that once independence was achieved, all else would follow. And poverty, as always, served to deny people a voice. The poor and illiterate are usually and conveniently silent.

It is true that Lenin, following J. A. Hobson, saw the poverty of India, China, and Africa as the counterpart of the affluence of the advanced industrial countries. People in the developed lands, including trade union members, rode on the backs of the impoverished masses of the colonial or dependent world. But this had no recognition in the accepted economic theory and the resulting attitudes and instruction. Malthus spoke to the impoverishing pressure of population growth, but it was with Europe that he was primarily concerned. It was simply agreed that some countries were naturally poor as others were naturally unhealthy. There were exceptions to this way of dismissing the problem to which I will come later. But they were only exceptions to the general tendency.

At the beginning of his new term in 1949, President Harry S. Truman committed the United States to his now famous Point IV, a promise of a bold program to place the technical resources and achievements of the United States at the service of the less fortunate people of the world. It was a step in direct descent from the Marshall Plan, which by then was showing great promise in the restoration of European economic life. There was one improvement; technical assistance, as distinct from capital, seemed to promise progress at a much lower price. In the early weeks of 1949, I served on a State Department committee which sought to give content to the President's promise, for, as often before and since, the rhetoric of intention had run ahead of the design for action. Rarely can deliberations have been more unstructured. None of the concerned officials or outside experts had strong views as to the needs of the poor countries or what one or another form of technical assistance would accomplish. There was very little literature to which we could refer. The tactful euphemisms for poverty – less developed countries, LDCs, developing countries, the Third World – had not been invented. One member of the committee, Paul H. Nitze, later to win distinction as an influential and predictable Cold Warrior, was moved to argue that little if any substance could be given to the President's proposal – there was no practical way of ameliorating the poverty of the poor countries by public action. More routine officials agreed with as much haste as was seemly. Had it not been for the firmness of the presidential commitment and even more the spontaneity of the resulting public response, the negative men would, I then felt, have carried the day.

It is a vivid lesson on the emptiness of this economic box. There was also ample evidence to the same effect in the universities. I had previously given thought to the considerable number of students coming to Harvard from the poor countries under one scholarship arrangement or another to study economics, who were now studying the sophisticated models applicable, if at all, only to the United States and the other advanced industrial countries. Partly as a result and partly in consequence of the interest stirred by the Point IV proposals, I began instruction in the economics of poverty and economic development at Harvard, in company with some talented younger associates.[1] It was very nearly the first such instruction in the United States.

We were again oppressed by a nearly total absence of intellectually acceptable material for our students to

1. These were Richard Holton, later Professor and Dean of the College of Business Administration at the University of California at Berkeley; Carolyn Bell, later a professor at Wellesley College and a leading exponent of the right of women to teach economics; and Gustav Papanek, now of Boston University, who has made the problems of the poor countries his lifetime concern. In these years, with the support of the Carnegie Corporation, I also began a book provisionally entitled *Why People Are Poor*. Its concern was less with mass poverty than with residual poverty in the rich countries. With the passage of time, I came to concentrate not on the causes of poverty but on the nature of affluence and the reasons why in the affluent country a minority was left behind in squalor and deprivation. In keeping with this dialectic, the book eventually emerged under the title *The Affluent Society*.

read, and, when I petitioned my then-older colleagues for approval of economic development as one of the fields which students might present for the Ph.D., my request was promptly and, in keeping with accepted academic style, rather righteously rejected. As a different field of study, the special economics of the poor countries was held not to exist.

In the next fifteen years in the United States these attitudes were decisively reversed. Aid to the poor countries by the United States, negligible in 1950, was in excess of $5·5 billion in 1965.[2] Over a somewhat longer period, the Ford Foundation contributed well over a billion dollars between 1950 and 1975, and the Rockefeller, Carnegie, and some CIA-supported foundations added smaller amounts.[3] Several thousand people were publicly and privately engaged in giving or administering assistance to the poor countries in this general period. Intellectual interest in the problem of mass poverty had also greatly expanded. Seminars and courses on economic development had proliferated in universities and colleges across the land. At Harvard the earlier principles had yielded to the pressures of students, money, and academic fashion; economic

2. *Economic Report of the President, 1966* (Washington, D.C.: U.S. Government Printing Office. 1966), pp. 140–70. This is the total of all non-European, non-military aid, including Food for Peace, Export-Import Bank loans, and subscriptions to capital funds of international lending agencies.

3. Francis X. Sutton, 'American Foundations and Public Management in Developing Countries', A Ford Foundation Reprint, 1977, p. 6. Reprinted from 'Education and Training for Public Sector Management in the Developing Countries', Rockefeller Foundation, March 1977.

development had become a full-fledged field of speciali-
zation, as at all other universities decently abreast of the
times. A properly motivated (and financed) scholar could
attend as many as half a dozen conferences a year on the
subject in the United States, at the United Nations, and
in foreign countries far and near. Some did. No
economic subject more quickly captured the attention
of so many as the rescue of the people of the poor countries from their poverty.

The sources of this interest were several. One, with
roots in the colonial era, reflected the compassionate
hope of more fortunate people that they might do something for the poor. Many more Spanish, French, Dutch,
and British colonial officials, not to mention mis-
sionaries, medical and otherwise, were concerned in
their time with bringing the benefits (as they saw them)
of law, irrigation, education, railroad transportation,
religion, and personal hygiene to the people of their
subject countries than a more cynical or ideologically
inclined age now concedes.

The years from 1950 to 1965 were also ones of major
economic success and self-approval in the United States
and the other industrial countries. It may have occurred
to some far-sighted scholars that, were this to continue,
the economic problem would disappear, and economists
would become obsolete. Keynes had warned of this
danger: 'the economic problem is not – if we look into
the future – *the permanent problem of the human race.*'[4] To be

4. John Maynard Keynes, 'Economic Possibilities for Our
Grandchildren' in *Essays in Persuasion* (London: Rupert Hart-
Davis 1952) p. 366. (This was first published in 1931.) The em-
phasis is in the original.

involved with the poor countries provided the scholar with a foothold in a field of study that would assuredly expand and endure.

More important, certainly, was seeming strategic interest. This had two aspects. There was the belief, perhaps more properly again the instinct, that if the poor countries remained in wretched and painful deprivation, the rich countries would not be safe in their comfortable affluence. 'We cannot create a heaven inside and leave a hell outside and expect to survive,' Clement Attlee said in his notable warning as prime minister when speaking of the great decolonization effort of his administration. His words were widely echoed. The rich countries were not strongly attracted by the idea of giving up their wealth. Therefore the poor must be made less poor.

More compelling than this dialectic was the fear of Communism. It was accepted in the 1950s that, if the poor countries were not rescued from their poverty, the Communists would take over.[5] In 1952, Adlai Steven-

5. Some justifications of this belief have a stridently archaic ring. Here is that of Jacob J. Kaplan. a former senior official of the Department of State and the Agency for International Development: 'The U.S. national security interest in developing nations appears to fall into four categories: (1) rebuffing Communist threats to take them over by overt or covert aggression; (2) using their military forces and territory for reinforcing U.S. ability to defend both its own land areas and others threatened by Communist aggression; (3) minimizing conflicts among developing nations; and (4) the propagation of congenial values and institutions, however much they may vary from U.S. norms, to suit the conditions and traditions of poorer societies.' *The Challenge of Foreign Aid: Policies, Problems. and Possibilities* (New York: Frederick A. Praeger, 1967), pp. 109-10.

33

son attacked Republicans who would rather talk about who had lost China than how to save India. 'It would seem to me, my friends, that the Republican critics could better demonstrate the good faith of their concern for Asia by doing something about India and Pakistan today rather than talking about China yesterday.'[6] In what was otherwise no springtime for liberals – the years of Joseph R. McCarthy and John Foster Dulles – one could be for help to the poor of the world and explain that it was not suspect compassion but hard-boiled anti-Communism. Even principled conservatives conceded this need, although the most principled remained with the belief that anything as insidious as Communism should be put down by forthright military action. In his inaugural address on 20 January 1961, John F. Kennedy questioned the identification of the concern for poverty with anti-Communism by saying, 'To those peoples in the huts and villages of half the globe struggling to break the bonds of mass misery, we pledge our best effort to help them help themselves, for whatever period is required – not because the Communists may be doing it, not because we seek their votes, but because it is right.' He, too, echoed Attlee: 'If a free society cannot help the many who are poor, it cannot save the few who are rich.'[7]

Concern for Communism in the poor countries was a major aberration of the foreign-policy and strategic

6. *Major Campaign Speeches of Adlai E. Stevenson* (New York: Random House, 1953), p. 97.

7. *The Inaugural Addresses of the American Presidents from Washington to Kennedy*, annotated by Davis Newton Lott (New York: Holt, Rinehart and Winston, 1961), p. 270.

mind, based on two beliefs of pervasive influence and minimal substance. One was that, in the absence of effective development under non-Communist auspices, the Communists would forthwith take over. The second was that the Communist development would then be ruthless and successful and the country in question would soon become a power – military and economic – in the world balance between capitalism and socialism.

Had it indeed been so, the Communist alternative would have been irresistible. In practical fact, Communism was not an alternative; its intense administrative requirements were and remain, the exceptional case of China apart, well beyond the limited administrative competence and experience of the new country. And even if this problem is mastered or partly mastered, poverty continues. So do economic, political, and military weakness. The countries about which there was so much concern would be, under any economic and political system, minor factors in all conventional strategic calculations for decades to come.

Yet strategic anti-Communism remained important in American policy, and eventually with results as disastrous as any in our history. With the rise of Communism in Indo-China, Vietnam in particular, there was a general difference of view as to whether it should be countered by economic, technical, and social efforts to ameliorate hardship and economic injustice or by military action or by what combination of the two. Liberals leaned to economic amelioration, conservatives to military measures. Until the late sixties, the debate on the Vietnam war was mostly on means, not on the need for American action or intervention. Having committed themselves to economic development as an antidote for Communism, liberals did not easily develop skepticism about the enterprise as a whole.

Specifically, the question of whether the United States could shape and guide political development in a country culturally and geographically so removed from itself did not for a long time get asked. Nor was there much inquiry as to whether we needed to try – whether the nature of the economic and political system of what would long be a weak, small economy and polity affected in any important way any visible interest of the United States. Failure to understand the nature of mass poverty and, more precisely, a misunderstanding of its relation to Communist opportunity or the limits thereof were central in the greatest disaster in American foreign policy.

The explosion of concern over the condition of the poor nations in the 1950s and 1960s, the increase in assistance and the associated political debate, the large increase in the number of people actually and officially concerned with the problem, and, eventually, the explicit imperatives of Vietnam, where a policy intended to forestall or contain Communism was under immediate and awful test, all pointed, and desperately, to the same need. That was for agreement, explicit or implied, on the causes of poverty. There had to be action; the commitment to this was powerful. But if there was to be a remedy, there had to be a cause. If it couldn't otherwise be identified, it would have to be invented or assumed. We suppose that on social questions we proceed from diagnosis to action. But if action is imperative, we make the cause fit the action. So it was here. To recognize this is absolutely fundamental to an understanding of the policy against poverty in the two decades following the Second World War and of the causes of poverty that are still put forward. The imperatives of action specified the causes that were not acceptable, and they selected the causes that were.

The most obvious of the possible causes of poverty that had to be excluded was the economic system. Were mass poverty the result of a socially or economically exploitative or oppressive system, the remedy would be to sweep it away - to eliminate the landlords, capitalists, feudal governing or exploiting classes that held the people in poverty. But this could not be a cause, for it meant that Communism or what could be so described was the cure. Few who reflect on this cause will insist that it is independent of remedy. One can perhaps be sorry that in poor, rural societies Communism and socialism do not often - as Marx himself urged - have great relevance or remedial value. Deprivation would quickly end were it so.

The exigencies of policy also excluded other causes. Climate could not be cited. Nothing much from Washington could be done about that. In any case, political tact excluded any suggestion that, as a result of hot weather, people were torpid or shiftless. Ethnic character was similarly excluded. Bengalis could not yet be converted into Punjabis or Chinese. Tact again intervened on the side of what most would consider good anthropology. Similarly, if there are scientifically valid distinctions between different national and ethnic communities, they grow out of differing experiences of government, family traditions, religion, and education. But these are part of the history of a particular people. And history is singularly unchangeable after it is made.

For a long period in the 1950s, demographic factors – the pressure of population on land resources and food supply – could not be a cause of poverty. That was because the remedy was birth control, and this risked the alienation of the Catholics of the developed world. Not until the late fifties, when a commission established by President Eisenhower under the chairmanship of the late William Draper declared that uncontrolled population increases were a major source of deprivation and needed to be checked, did this cause of poverty become officially acceptable. The most relentlessly Malthusian country in the world is India. It is also the one to which, in the two decades following the Second World War, the United States accorded the greatest assistance. Until I went there in 1961, no senior American official had, to my knowledge, adverted seriously in public to birth control as an indispensable element in any attack on mass poverty. I did so not out of courage but in accordance with the calculation that, if there were protests from Catholics, a Catholic president was uniquely equipped to deal with his co-religionists. In fact, there was no objection, perhaps partly because I was not heard.[8]

8. I was encouraged by another incident as interesting as it was uncalculated. In 1962, Mrs Jacqueline Kennedy visited India. One day, returning from a visit to the All-India Institute of Medical Sciences, she surveyed the masses of children who had been released from school in her honor and in deference to their own curiosity. She was more appalled than pleased by the numbers. She said, 'I hope the fact that we're Catholic isn't keeping anyone [meaning any American] from advocating birth control.'

To this day, emphasis on population pressure as a cause of poverty is somewhat muted. This is partly because any resulting improvement is long delayed. Causes that seem to yield more rapidly to results are favored.[9] But also, as with climate, there is the problem of tact. To advise the poor, especially if black, to remedy their situation by reducing their numbers will, it is feared, invite an adverse response.

In contrast, the circular causes of poverty – those where cause and result are interchangeable – and the related actions were often agreeable to those urging them. Professional educators – retired deans of schools of education despatched by ECA and AID – readily attributed poverty to the absence of an educational system. And former civil servants attributed it to poor public administration. Many so qualified took up residence in Third World capitals to propose and guide improvement. Without resources to spend on education, not much could, in fact, be done to improve education. And the case is the same with public administration. Potential teachers and administrators from the poor country could be brought to the United States or Europe for training. This remedy also recommended itself because it was and remains greatly popular with those who hope to be selected. A very large number of those so prepared do not return more than momentarily to their own countries, for this particular course and solution facilitates what presently we shall see is the most practiced but least celebrated remedy for poverty.

9. I regard birth control measures as worthy of the strongest emphasis. I do not deal with them in any detail here, for they are in a different time dimension as regards effect from the forces influencing the equilibrium of poverty which I do consider.

That is for the motivated to serve themselves by moving from the poor countries to the rich. This movement, in its long-run effect, is not adverse to economic advance and, as we shall see, has more often been greatly favorable. But it is not the result that those emphasizing education had in mind.

As often in economics, choice had narrowed in a cruel way. The rich countries had technical skills in abundance. So the cause of mass poverty was seen as technical backwardness in methods of production. This was a particularly attractive cause, for the remedial action, the supply of technical expertise, was, as earlier observed, not expensive. But the rich countries, as an aspect of their wealth, also had capital. And few improvements in production methods are possible without capital investment, a matter to which I will return. So a shortage of capital also became a cause of poverty and its supply a remedy. In the great explosion of concern over poverty, we did not, to repeat, move from cause to remedy; we moved from the only available line of remedial action to the cause that called for that action.

It was easier than might be imagined. In the rich countries capital investment and technical innovation are related to rising real income. There is a powerful temptation in economics to believe that such experience is of universal application.

It helped, also, that the cause selected by the available remedy was economic, which meant that economists were principally involved. Ours is a profession that is notably skilled in assuming away inconvenient causation. 'Economists are generous in stating general reservations about the importance of "non-economic" factors, without, however, letting this change their approach.'[10] Reputations here, as elsewhere in the social sciences, can be advanced by patient refinement of detail within the larger framework of assumptions. The last can remain more or less indefinitely unquestioned. So it was here.

Also the rapid increase in the numbers of people concerned with economic development did not guarantee the highest level of talent. Both public officials and scholars brought to the field by the expansion of interest after 1950 had a tendency at the highest level to allow faith to be a substitute for critical judgement. At a lower level, jobs were involved. Judgement, even of a refined and scholarly sort, is more readily made subordinate to self-interest than we commonly imagine or, in polite discourse, assert.

As sufficiently stated, diagnosis that proceeds from the available remedy does not inspire confidence. And the results of the current considerable effort and greater interest, though not negligible, have certainly fallen short of expectation. In the countries of mass poverty – India, Pakistan, Bangladesh, Indonesia, large parts of Africa and Latin America – the deprivation remains extensively unabated and unchanged.[11] In the rich

10. Gunnar Myrdal, *Asian Drama: An Inquiry Into the Poverty of Nations*, abridged ed. (New York: Pantheon, 1971), p. 15.

11. 'In spite of the tremendous economic progress of the last twenty years [in the world at large], the promise of effective development is dimmed by the fact that very little progress has been made by the poorest peoples and nations . . . It has been estimated that

countries a mood of resignation and detachment has partly replaced the earlier hope. Few will resist the thought that a further, maybe different, look at the causes of mass poverty could be in order.

---

over 700 million people exist in conditions of absolute poverty . . . [T]here are additional millions who live just above marginal subsistence.' Poverty is here defined in terms of serious caloric deficiency. 'Development Co-operation', Report by Maurice J. Williams in the 1977 *Review* of the Organization for Economic Co-operation and Development (Paris: November 1977), pp. 8–9.

3

The Equilibrium of Poverty

Mass poverty of the kind seen in rural Tamil Nadu and elsewhere cannot be viewed as a 'pocket phenomenon' or as a
mere aberration of the system. It is a reflection of the total
malfunctioning of the economic order . . . Hence any attempt
to analyse the problem in terms of one or two variables such
as low capital formation or absence of policy measures to
ensure adequate distribution of income must be viewed with
suspicion . . . There is no comprehensive theory which details
the working of an economy such as that of Tamil Nadu.[1]

The accepted diagnosis of mass poverty – insufficient
capital, backward technology – went beyond its
strategic convenience. It had also the blessing of the
most reputable economic thought. What was recommended for the poor countries was what had served,
and seemed still to serve, in the rich countries. No
serious and exacting thought was given to the possibility that *both* economic circumstance and economic
motivation might be fundamentally different in the

1. C. T. Kurien, 'Rural Poverty in Tamil Nadu' in *Poverty and
Landlessness in Rural Asia* (Geneva: International Labour Office,
1977), p. 127. Tamil Nadu is the former Madras state, with a
population in 1971 of more than 40 million.

poor country from such circumstance and motivation in the rich. In particular, the normal tendency of the rich country could be to expanding output and income. And the assurance of the resulting reward would then affect aspiration – what the beneficiaries, reflecting on the pleasures of more personal income, refer to in resounding terms as incentives. If one has some certainty of getting more, it will be worth trying to get more.

In the poor country, by contrast, the tendency could be to an equilibrium of poverty. An increase in income could set in motion the forces that would eliminate the increase and restore the previous level of deprivation. Improvement could devour itself.

And it is far from unreasonable to suppose that so malign a tendency would have an effect on motivation. Motivation, like so much else, is subject to conditioning by its culture. If forces, great or overwhelming, act to inhibit or exclude economic improvement, will not people – some, if not all – abandon the struggle?

What seems plausible is real. The tendency of the rich country *is* to increasing income; the tendency of the poor country *is* to an equilibrium of poverty. And in each there is accommodation, in the one case to the fact of improvement, in the other to the hopelessness of the prospect. This is the difference at the extremes. As always in economics, differences are of degree; between the rich country and the poor are many intermediate shadings. But at the extremes the differences are stark. To these differences and their origins, I now turn.

*

The factors making for improved material well-being in the rich countries of the non-Communist world are matters of general agreement. Disagreement arises not in the identification of the elements of progress but in the weight to be accorded the individual items and how they should be given expression. This is in a tradition of economic thought that gained initial impetus with Adam Smith, was further and greatly developed early in the last century by David Ricardo and Thomas Robert Malthus, was put in near modern form just before the beginning of the present century by Alfred Marshall, and was subsequently amended by John Maynard Keynes. Its essentials were: savings over current consumption to purchase capital; a progressive technology to embody or make use of the capital; a political and social system that allows and encourages the individual to seek his (or her) own betterment; and a regulation of the whole process, in the main by the market. For Ricardo and Malthus improvement in the well-being of workers, as distinct from that of the community as a whole, required that they limit their numbers - that they not breed up to the limits of their subsistence. And on this neither Ricardo nor Malthus saw any real hope of success - Malthus urged as a solution that ministers, while performing the marriage ceremony, warn of the adverse consequences of unrestrained intercourse. But, in time, it became evident that in the higher stages of economic development people would, with great reliability, limit their numbers and that scientific and technological advance would enable people to maximize sexual enjoyment while minimizing the procreative result.

45

Concern over population growth then ceased to be economic in any decisive sense. It survived residually as a problem of space and environment. Instead, in a general way, there was concern for the quality of the human stock as this served economic expansion. Expenditures on health care and education came to be referred to as investment in human capital. The terminology served also to proclaim, to the considerable advantage of physicians, educators and others, that these outlays served the same purpose as investment in diesel engines or nuclear reactors. Accordingly, their cost and return were subject to seemingly as hard-nosed an economic calculation as that for plant and machinery, to which they were not clearly inferior in economic value.

Additionally, among the requisites of improving well-being in the rich countries, there was the need to ensure that advance would not be interrupted or reversed – specifically, that business depressions would be prevented or offset. With Keynes in the years of the Great Depression came agreement or near-agreement that governments should intervene as needed to maintain a level of aggregate demand that would employ all or nearly all of the available labor force and maintain pressure for a continuing expansion of plant capacity.

Such are the accepted requisites of improving well-being in the rich countries. As noted, only on the relative importance of these several requirements do the growth models beloved by the economists of the established or neo-classical tradition engender debate. Capital supply, technology to embody it, education, even the regulation of aggregate demand, are equally intrinsic components of socialist well-being.

Blessed by the capitalist industrial world and extensively graced by socialist thought, it is easy to see why the elements of the remedies for poverty just mentioned seemed universal. There was further affirmation from experience – a useful thing. Progress in the advanced industrial countries had for decades, even centuries, come to be considered normal. And in the years following the Second World War, the measurement of economic product and income and their distribution made this improvement a matter of everyday discussion. A country with a low rate of growth – Britain was the depressing case – was regarded as exceptional as well as slightly depraved. Growth was normal, and social virtue lay with the greatest rate of growth.

This improvement, in combination with a declining rate of population increase, almost certainly had its effect on aspiration. Many, if not most, people could look forward to improving real income in most years. They could aspire to progressive increases in income in the knowledge that most likely they would get them. Some assurance of reward is surely essential for effort; motivation is a function of success. The chance for improvement and the resulting motivation being present in the rich countries, they were then assumed to be present in the poor.

It was a grievous miscalculation.

A first, if obvious, feature of mass poverty must be emphasized; it is, overwhelmingly, a rural affliction. That is because the elementary requisites of existence – food, clothing, and basic shelter – all come from the land. The mass urban poverty of the poor country, that

47

of Calcutta, Cairo, Mexico City, is a relatively modern phenomenon, a development of the last fifty or seventy-five years. It is not benign. It is, however, one step up from rural deprivation. That is why these cities have grown. In the United States, as elsewhere in the world, it is not always seen that life in a meager rural cabin, with only the most elementary food and clothing, slight educational opportunity, no health care, and much social discrimination, can be worse than life in any urban ghetto. And urban poverty, the world over, is not the typical manifestation of deprivation. The poor of India, Bangladesh, Pakistan, Indonesia, Egypt, nearly all of Africa, and much of Latin America are still, to the extent of 70 to 80 per cent of the total population – much of Africa even more – in the rural villages.[2] It is, accordingly, on rural poverty that attention must be centered.

It is rural poverty, also, that is intractable. Here people have lived at or near the minimum necessary for survival for a long time; for practical purposes, always. And here the condition persists because they live in an equilibrium of poverty. Few things allow of escape from life at a minimum level of subsistence; when something does, there are forces which operate to return the people to something approaching their former level of depri-

2. 'Three-quarters of the people of the developing world live in rural areas and the bulk of extreme poverty, about 80 per cent, is found there. Most of the extremely poor are in Asia and Africa, but even in Latin America poverty is primarily a rural problem.' 'Development Co-operation', Report by Maurice J. Williams in the 1977 *Review* of the Organization for Economic Co-operation and Development (Paris: November 1977), p. 12.

vation. Improving income here is not normal. It is and always has been unknown.

It is the equilibrium of rural poverty which evokes, as an explanation, the hitherto mentioned circular causation. Since life is near the bare level of subsistence, there is no saving. Without saving and the resulting capital investment, there can be, from within the agricultural economy itself, no investment in improved agricultural technology – in irrigation, hybrid seeds, pesticides, fertilizer, improved machine cultivation. Without such investment there can be no improvement in income that allows of saving and further investment.

It will be suggested that in nearly all communities there are some people with some surplus for saving. This is so, but the meagerness of capital supply remains a ruling fact. It will also be urged that improvements in technology are possible that require no appreciable investment. These could be less available than is commonly imagined. In October 1953, a young Cornell anthropologist, W. David Hopper, took up residence in the village of Senapur in northern India and for the next fifteen months studied its agricultural economy in intelligent detail. He concluded that, given the absence of investment resources, agricultural technology in the village was at or near the optimum. 'An observer in Senapur cannot help but be impressed with the way the village uses its physical resources. The age-old techniques have been refined and sharpened by countless years of experience, and each generation seems to have had its experimenters who added a bit here and changed a practice there, and thus improved the community lore.'[3] Other scholars have reached broadly similar conclusions.[4] This impression of optimal technical achievement, given the resources that are available, is substantially at odds with the accepted beliefs of agricultural education, especially in the United States, conclusions that are again heavily influenced by the available remedy. Also, if one's trade is supplying agricultural advice, one must believe it is useful. Such advice being available and inexpensive, such belief becomes the basis of policy. However, the possibility of technical improvement with small investment cannot be excluded. High-yielding hybrids are an obvious case, although investment in fertilizer and very frequently in water supply is necessary to realize anything approaching their full potential. And before coming to the social resistance to change, there is another highly practical consideration which excludes it.

That is the nature of risk calculation in the poor community. All innovation involves, or will be deemed to involve, a certain risk of failure. This, it may be noted, is always higher for the cultivator who adopts it than for the expert who recommends it. But risk has a special dimension of urgency in the present context. For

3. W. David Hopper, 'The Economic Organization of a Village in North Central India' (Ph.D. diss., Cornell University, 1957). Cited by Theodore W. Schultz, *Transforming Traditional Agriculture* (New Haven: Yale University Press, 1964), p. 45.

4. See Schultz, pp. 48–52. Mention should be made of the noted study by John Lossing Buck of Chinese agriculture, *Chinese Farm Economy* (Chicago: University of Chicago Press, 1930). It was Dr Buck's agricultural teaching and research in China that took Pearl Buck, his wife at the time, to that country with deep consequences, however ambiguous as to quality, for modern literature.

the affluent Western farmer, crop failure means loss of income. This is disagreeable, but it does not often involve physical deprivation, certainly never life itself. And it is thus that Western agriculturalists, practicing and professional, tend to regard risk and that the professional advisers recommend technical change. To the family that lives on the margin of subsistence, however, failure means hunger, possibly death. So regarded, risk is not something to be accepted casually. Among the very poor, risk aversion, as it is called by economists, is very high – and for reasons that are wholly rational.[5]

But rural poverty has a yet more vital aspect, one deserving of further emphasis. Its equilibrium, if broken, will normally be restored. If new investment or new technology, however acquired, increases income, forces will normally be set in motion that restore the previous or some other stable level of deprivation. If income increases for any other reason, the income will not be self-perpetuating. The tendency will be to a new equilibrium, and this, quite possibly, will be at or near the previous level of income. The increase will, in effect, consume itself.

In northern and western India in the last century, the British built vast irrigation works to supplement the insufficient or uncertain rainfall. The acreage so irrigated is still by far the most extensive on the globe. Canal digging for thousands of people on the northern

5. A point emphasized by the late Michal Kalecki, the brilliant Polish economist to whose innovative thought all of his friends, of whom I, fortunately, was one, have a greater debt than they can easily acknowledge.

Indus Plain became a way of life, handed down from father to son. And the British also invested heavily in railroads that allowed of a more efficient and equitable distribution of available food resources across the land – much Indian railroad-building was a famine-relief measure.

This massive investment came from outside the immediate rural household; it could not have been accomplished from resources saved voluntarily from within. It was admirably designed to enhance the income of the millions affected. The result of this investment was the survival of people who would otherwise have died, the birth of children who would not otherwise have been born. In further consequence, there was an increase in population, which, since the increased food supply and associated income had to be shared, returned people to or near the previous level of deprivation and restored the equilibrium of poverty. If people's lives are being shortened by malnutrition or famine or if they are not breeding because they are sick or dead, the first inevitable effect of any escape from poverty is to save lives, including the lives of those who, in consequence of a manageable proposition in biology, would not be born because their parents would be dead. This escape, however humane, restores the equilibrium of poverty.

Poverty has a further hold on the poor. In the affluent country improving income leads to increased saving and investment. This saving is enhanced because it is extensively protected from the pressures of personal consumption; the decision to save and invest is made in largest part not by individuals who have the alternative of expenditure for consumer needs but *for* them by corporations. In consequence of this investment and improving technology, there can be and regularly are increasing returns to labor – later workers add more to product than those before.

In the poor country any improvement in income is nakedly exposed to the pressures of consumption, and these pressures, needless to say, poverty makes infinitely more urgent. So saving and investment are minimized while, as noted, improved technology usually requires investment. So added workers from the increased population have a progressively lower yield. The law of secular diminishing returns can be indefinitely postponed in its operation in the rich country. It still works inexorably in the poor rural community.[6]

So, to summarize, the poverty of the poor country denies its people the means for improvement. And if these become available, there are built into the structure of poverty the social and biological forces by which improvement is aborted, the poverty perpetuated.

In the rich country, in contrast, circumstances are not only different, they are very nearly the reverse. Here incomes are higher than the minimum necessary for adequate nutrition and health and, for many, high enough to be disabling; here also the largest share of all saving is by corporations and thus protected from the pressures of consumption. So saving and investment come easily, even automatically. For this reason, population increase in the rich countries can yield increasing returns. And, in any case, the birth-rate is under con-

6. A tendency strongly affirmed by the I LO study, *Poverty and Landlessness in Rural Asia.*

trol, and the death rate does not respond to improved well-being. A world of difference thus divides the two cases – in one case, an equilibrium of poverty and, in the other, the protected dynamic of change. But this may not be the greatest difference. The more important difference is in acculturation – in accommodation to the culture of poverty.

4

Accommodation

In the rich country a large proportion of the people have come to expect a comfortable and also an increasing income. This is a circumstance to which they have accommodated their thoughts and expectations. An effort, general though by no means universal, to improve income is assumed. Most significantly, it is assumed by economists and other scholars. There is broad accommodation to the idea of increasing income.

It should not surprise us then, though it does, that the poor also accommodate to their poverty. And especially so the rural poor. This tendency to accommodation is a fact of the greatest importance.

We have observed the forces making for an equilibrium of poverty - that make poverty self-perpetuating and restore the previous level of deprivation, or something approaching it, if there is temporary improvement. But nothing so reinforces this equilibrium as the absence of aspiration - the absence of effort to escape it. In the poor rural community such aspiration, in turn, is in conflict with one of the most profound and predictable elements of human behavior. That is the refusal to struggle against the impossible, the tendency to prefer acquiescence to frustration.

People who have lived for centuries in poverty in the relative isolation of the rural village have come to terms with this existence. It would be astonishing were it otherwise. People do not strive, generation after generation, century after century, against circumstances that are so constituted as to defeat them. They accept. Nor is such acceptance a sign of weakness of character. Rather, it is a profoundly rational response. Given the formidable hold of the equilibrium of poverty within which they live, accommodation is the optimal solution. Poverty is cruel. A continuing struggle to escape that is continuously frustrated is more cruel. It is more civilized, more intelligent, as well as more plausible, that people, out of the experience of centuries, should reconcile themselves to what has for so long been the inevitable.

The deeply rational character of accommodation lies back, at least in part, of the central instruction of the principal world religions. All, without exception, urge acquiescence, some in remarkably specific form. The blessedness that Christianity accords to the meek is categorical. The pain of poverty is not denied, but its compensatory spiritual reward is very high. The poor pass through the eye of the needle into Paradise; the rich remain outside with the camels. Acquiescence is equally urged, or as in the case of Hinduism compelled, by the other ancient faiths. There has long been a suspicion, notably enhanced by Marx, that the contentment urged by religion is a design for diverting attention from the realities of class and exploitation – it is the opiate of the people. It is, more specifically, a formula for making the best of a usually hopeless situation.

56

The ethical judgment of the affluent community, as well as its economics, is thought appropriate to the poor. Accordingly and instinctively, the rich community reacts derogatorily to the accommodation of the poor to their poverty; here are people who deserve no sympathy, for they do not even try. This again reflects a serious failure of understanding, another example of the highly inappropriate transfer of the highly conditioned attitudes of the rich country to the poor.

Even in the poorest country, where the grip of the poverty equilibrium is most binding, accommodation is not complete. There is always a minority which seeks to escape. And, as the possibility of escape increases, the logic and rationality of accommodation decline. So the proportion rejecting accommodation and making the effort to escape increases. Countries lie in a continuum between the extremes of general mass poverty and relative mass affluence. As one proceeds from the extreme of poverty to that of relative affluence, the hold of the equilibrium of poverty is relaxed, to be replaced by the dynamic of improvement. Accommodation does not disappear; the tendency to accept, to be content with an accustomed living standard, persists. It persists, however, in a progressively smaller share of the population.

In the farming community in southern Ontario in which I spent my youth, the struggle for economic improvement was held to be general. This was as the folk mythology required. The farmers were of Scottish descent; the Scotch (as they were called) were known by all to be very enterprising people. In fact, many, perhaps a majority, lived in relatively well-nourished penury, with full acceptance that this was their intended fate. Rural Ontario differed from rural India in the higher level of physical well-being at which accommodation occurred and the very much larger proportion of the people rejecting accommodation, reflecting, in turn, the much greater ease of such escape.

A practical manifestation of accommodation has long been important for the work of agricultural extension services and similar agencies of agricultural improvement in the advanced countries. The most effective work of these agencies was with a minority of farmers, and it was noticed, not without some sense of guilt and failure, that these were usually the most progressive and prosperous, the ones who seemed least to need the help. Those most in need remained the most stolidly with their accustomed methods of cultivation or husbandry or changed only slowly in response to the example of their progressive neighbors. For a generation or more after the establishment of the extension service early in this century, county agents rarely gathered in conference or convention without lamenting the fact that most of their farmer clients, and especially the neediest, did not seek to improve or seek the income that went with improvement.

Though regarded as unworthy and even unnatural, accommodation was thus fully recognized. The practical importance of such recognition in the poor countries, as we shall see presently, is, if anything, much greater. It leads to emphasis on attacking accommodation as a prerequisite to agricultural improvement. And it strongly urges the concentration of resources on the minority, however small, which has rejected accommodation. Both of these matters involve an important break with past practice.

The notion of accommodation has very little standing in the literature of economic development. There has been comment on some of its manifestations – the stubborn commitment of some of the North American Indian communities to their traditional mode of life is a prominent example. And 'absence of motivation' is frequently cited in general terms as a barrier to development. Otherwise, explicit reference to accommodation as a natural and predictable response to poverty is rare.[1] Economists of both the advanced capitalist and socialist worlds take the will to improve for granted. Their recommendations are universally for

1. Along with risk aversion, it receives explicit statement in John W. Mellor's *The Economics of Agricultural Development* (Ithaca: Cornell University Press, 1966). pp. 244–5. 'A traditional agriculture tends to be dominated by an attitude which emphasizes survival and maintenance of position rather than improvement and advancement of position. Two features of a traditional agriculture encourage this attitude. First there is high risk associated with innovation . . . Second . . . a high penalty for error in innovation because the farmers' low income will not absorb a sharp drop before reaching the minimal requirements for subsistence.

'Over a period of time the economic advantage of conservatism often becomes institutionalized in religious strictures and other cultural traits . . .

. . . If farmers are fully content with their lot, they will not change present practices in order to increase production and income. Disinterest in improved material welfare may grow n a situation in which historically there has been no possibility of improved welfare through increased production.'

people who seek material improvement. If such improvement is not sought, the foundation that sustains all economic policy is gone. But clearly this cannot be conceded. No more than lawyers or undertakers are economists given to self-immolation. We too seek to keep alive the beliefs and myths that are essential for our profession.

Accommodation is also in conflict with affirmative policy. What legislature will vote money to save people from an existence to which they are reconciled? Also, to say that people have accommodated to their poverty seems derogatory – it dismisses them as unworthy, lacking in ambition or otherwise debased. Even if rational, accommodation does not seem an acceptable human tendency.

Finally, in the affluent countries the self-regarding rich for long used the contentment of the poor as the justification of the existing order: 'They are happy, poor things.' Charity or public assistance, the rich have argued, would only breed discontent and could be expensive, too. Civilized and compassionate people seek naturally to avoid the guilt of association with such doctrine.

Yet, not surprisingly, the accurate view, one that fully perceives the role of accommodation, has high practical utility. Poverty remains a painful thing whether people have accommodated to it or not. And to accept the fact of accommodation is not to accept the inevitability of poverty. Rather, along with an appreciation of the power of the grip of the poverty equilibrium, an understanding of accommodation explains why seemingly promising efforts at the relief of mass poverty have miscarried, been disappointing. And it shows how effort can be more effectively expended in the future. One source of disappointment which the equilibrium of poverty and the resulting accommodation allow us to understand is the often meager consequence of land reform.

To this point, discussion of the poverty of the rural community has involved major, even heroic, simplification. It has been as though no class structure were involved. All the poor have access to small landholdings and are kept in their poverty by the small product of the limited land resource available to them. In fact, all rural communities have a class structure. Among farm proprietors there are some with more land and some with less, although in such massively poor countries as India, Bangladesh, or Egypt the norm is not more but less. And, in practice, beneath the smallest proprietors there is always a class of landless laborers whose hold on existence is even more fragile than that of the poorest peasant. Above them all, in all the non-socialist countries with only the rarest exceptions, there is a landowning or landlord class which lives on revenues extracted in one form or another from those who work the land. These may be owners of considerable cultivable area who directly employ the landless laborers. Or they may be landlords who have the proprietors as tenants – and whose income is a share of the proceeds of the crop itself. Or, the common legacy of Spanish colonialism, the small proprietor obtains the right to cultivate his own plot by rendering service on the adjacent land of the landlord. The relationships

61

between the owner of land and those who work it are infinitely various, and they have lent themselves, over the years, to a precision of scholarly study which has gone far to conceal the circumstances that apply to all.

The common circumstance is a relationship of population to land which perpetuates the equilibrium of poverty even when landlordism is abolished. There are still, in all but the most atypical instances, too many people, too little land.

It is quite possible, as in Central America and elsewhere in Latin America, for landlords to extract enough income from tenants, even when these are excruciatingly poor, to provide a living standard for themselves that is far above that of the community in general. But the existence of such landlords does not alter the essential character of the equilibrium of poverty. There are still too many people. The mode of cultivation given by their numbers also excludes most innovation. Machinery must compete with negligible labor costs. And to bring in tractors and combine harvesters and expel the people may be considered dangerous even by an adequately insensitive landlord.

Meanwhile the equilibrium of poverty and more especially the resulting accommodation explain much that is otherwise inexplicable about land reform. Landlords, with privilege and income unrelated to any economic service or function, have survived in company with numerous and poor tenants and workers for centuries. Many still do. Not always, by any means, do they have the supporting power of police or soldiers. They have survived because the tenants have accommodated to their poverty. This, not their access to power, was the protection of the landed class.

The revolt against landed privilege, peaceful or otherwise, when it does come, is not without reward. Elimination of the differences in income, social prestige, and political power that go with landlordism can be a sufficient case in favor of such revolt. And so it has often been.[2] In China, South Korea, and Taiwan, land reform served these ends and also began an upward cycle of production. Elsewhere the economic improvement from land reform has been disappointing. That is because it so very rarely has broken the equilibrium of poverty. When redistributed to the tenants, the landlord's revenues have made little difference in their income. When income is negligible, it can be doubled and still be negligible. Such improvement as there may be is soon absorbed by the forces – higher survival rates, more births – that re-establish the previous equilibrium. Accommodation to the culture of poverty is also unchanged. This, in turn, reinforces the equilibrium of poverty by suppressing aspiration. So, after

2. A point on which Dudley Seers has spoken in language worth quoting: 'It is a truism that poverty will be eliminated much more rapidly if any given rate of economic growth is accompanied by a declining concentration of incomes. Equality should however be considered an objective in its own right ... Inequalities to be found now in the world, especially (but not only) outside the industrial countries, are objectionable by any religious or ethical standards. The social barriers and inhibitions of an unequal society distort the personalities of those with high incomes no less than of those who are poor. Trivial differences of accent, language, dress, customs, etc., acquire an absurd importance and contempt is engendered for those who lack social graces, especially country dwellers. Perhaps even more important, since race is usually highly correlated with income, economic inequality lies at the heart of racial tensions.' 'The Meaning of Development', *International Development Review* 11, no. 4 (1969).

land reform, economically at least, all is much as before.[3]

Generalization is rarely without exceptions. Although over most of history peasants have accommodated peacefully to their poverty and therewith to their landlords, it seems clear that, if pressed beyond a certain point, acceptance of landed power and privilege will dissolve. In Mexico, in 1911, Emiliano Zapata was able to arouse the peasants against the landlords. (One should note that that form of expression – arousing the peasants – sanctions accommodation as the normal situation.) Similarly Fidel Castro in Cuba. (It surely must have been one of the less forgivable miscalculations of the Bay of Pigs that it was thought that the Cubans wished to have the landlords back.) Following such a peasant revolt, the number who reject accommodation will, one imagines, also increase. This enhances change and improvement. And there have been instances, of which Cuba was again perhaps one, where the agriculture was so rich and efficient and the landowners and operators so affluent in their share that expropriation of the land and redistribution of income did make a difference.

But in Mexico after the destruction of the haciendas; as in the United States after the emancipation of the slaves; as in Russia after the freeing of the serfs or later after elimination of the landlords; and as in India after

3. A point on which I would disagree with the otherwise sympathetic views of Michael Harrington, *The Vast Majority: A Journey to the World's Poor* (New York: Simon and Schuster. 1977). pp. 228–9. Harrington sees more direct economic improvement from this general order of change than I think plausible.

the imposition of upper limits on allowable landhold-ings, the effect of the changed relation of people to land was not accompanied by the hoped-for improvement in income. For many there was no improvement at all. And this we now see was predictable. The changed relation of people to land did not alter the more endur-ing fact of an equilibrium of poverty and the accom-modation thereto.

5

What Is Now Explained

When the broad character of mass poverty is established – equilibrium, accommodation, rejection of accommodation by a minority – even the socially derogatory and scientifically unacceptable causes of poverty are found to make a useful contribution to the larger explanation.

Thus, in reflecting on the role of climate, scholars have rightly been suspicious of a simple relationship between the seasons and activity – cold weather and vigor; a hot, equable climate and physical and mental lassitude. But no one can reasonably doubt that the equilibrium of poverty can be established at a lower level of income in the tropics than in the temperate zone. It is also a reasonable hypothesis that diseases endemic to the tropics reinforce the equilibrium – the debilitating effects of malaria have long been recognized to have this result. The deprivation that is associated with the equilibrium and the associated diseases and disability is great. So, in consequence, is the number that will then survive and breed – and thus promptly restore the equilibrium of poverty – when food is temporarily abundant. It is a reasonable hypothesis, also, that the need in less hospitable climatic zones to supply clothing, store food, and construct shelter is an experience in the patterns of thought and activity which make the rejection of accommodation more likely. And the number rejecting accommodation to the equilibrium of poverty is, to repeat, a vital difference between rich countries and poor.

Similarly, the bearing of ethnic difference on poverty and well-being is explained. An ethnic community which has long been poor will have a strong accommodation to the equilibrium of poverty, and this acceptance will be relatively complete. One that has been less poor will have a less complete accommodation. More of its people will be seen as energetic or enterprising. But it will be to ethnic character, not historical experience and the resulting accommodation, that the difference between the two communities will be attributed.

India provides an admirable illustration of this tendency. As earlier noted, the peoples of eastern and southern India are said in everyday conversation to be poor because they are lacking in energy and ambition. This is in contrast with the energetic and ambitious peoples of the north and west who are significantly more affluent.

In fact, Bihar, Bengal, Orissa, and southern India have been caught in the equilibrium of poverty for centuries. In contrast, the Punjab in the last century was a region in rapid transition – vast irrigation works were built, accompanied by much fresh settlement and resettlement of the rural population. The independence of India and Pakistan then brought a huge migration into and out of the area. In consequence, the equilibrium of poverty has been appreciably less powerful in its grip there than elsewhere on the subcontinent. Likewise the associated accommodation. The so-called green revolution was a reality in Punjabi agriculture, and in the last couple of decades rural incomes have increased substantially.[1] In keeping with their higher income and their lesser accommodation, people of this region migrate in large numbers to the Indian cities and, to the extent possible, to foreign countries. These predictable tendencies are attributed not to the history of the people but to their being Punjabis. Had their accommodation to the culture of poverty over the centuries been the same as that of the people to the east and south, so, we may be sure, would be their ethnic reputation.

When the problem of poverty is viewed as here, the modern economic success of Hong Kong and Singapore also becomes explicable, as in lesser measure that of Taiwan and Israel. Again the explanation is not ethnic; Hong Kong and Singapore are merely the world's greatest assemblages of people who, rejecting accommodation, have escaped the equilibrium of poverty. The energy and thrust for accomplishment so aggregated and concentrated explains, far more than any other factor, the resulting development. Taiwan and Israel have similarly benefited from a large con-

1. Indira Rajaraman, 'Growth and Poverty in the Rural Areas of the Indian State of Punjab, 1960–61 to 1970–71' in *Poverty and Landlessness in Rural Asia* (Geneva: International Labour Office, 1977), pp. 61–74. In the Punjab, as elsewhere, the income of the very poorest fell.

centration of migrants similarly selected by their rejection of accommodation. In the vast rural areas of mainland China, the hold of the equilibrium of poverty remains strong, as also the accommodation thereto. However, none can doubt that the Chinese are bringing powerful efforts to bear on breaking the equilibrium of poverty (including a strong effort to counter the tendency for increasing population to devour improvement) and on the resulting accommodation.

The rejection of accommodation is not always voluntary. It can be forced, as it was on the Scottish tenants who were driven from the Highlands by the landlords and the sheep in the late eighteenth and early nineteenth centuries, and as it was on the Irish by the famine. It was similarly forced on large numbers of Indians and Pakistanis, as just mentioned, at the time of independence. Millions were so broken from accommodation - though in most cases accommodation to a level of living well above the Asian level - in Eastern Europe after the Second World War. Germany, like other recipients of such migrations, was greatly the beneficiary, something that, characteristically, has not been fully recognized. On few matters in our time are we determinedly so obtuse as on the way, in the rich countries, we look with misgiving on developments that select for us the people best designed to advance affluence. The German experience was peculiarly persuasive for my own view on these matters. It merits a brief digression.

In the summer and autumn of 1950, a joint American-German commission was constituted to study the problems of refugees in West Germany and to recommend amelioration. The commission was headed by the late Hans Christian Sonne, a liberal businessman and banker of wide-ranging public interests. I was appointed a member. We began meetings in Germany in the autumn of 1950 in the rather tense months following the outbreak of the Korean War.

In the aftermath of the Second World War, mostly in 1945 and 1946, upwards of 8 million persons came to, or were left stranded in, West Germany. Included were those who had come from or failed to return to East Germany, those expelled from the areas transferred to Poland and the Soviet Union, those expelled from the Sudetenland and the other Volksdeutschen communities in Eastern Europe. All seemed committed to a life of despair in their new and often inhospitable land, which also had more than its own share of economic problems. It was this seemingly mass consignment of people to poverty that had led to the forming of the commission.

For solving the problem of the refugees and other displaced persons, the commission could not have been more acutely timed. The problem was on the point of solving itself. Their previous accommodation shattered, the refugees had set about reestablishing themselves with energy and resourcefulness – and with a clear image in mind of the mode of life to which they had previously accommodated. The special problem of housing apart, most were well on their way. Workers from Silesia were at work in the mills and mines of the Ruhr. The small business craftsmen from Czechoslovakia were again in business in Bavaria and were again living in accustomed fashion, or would be when houses were built. Similarly farm hands and white-collar workers, as also members of the professions. The only large group that had not achieved its former living standard or seemed unlikely soon to do so were those whose living had derived from traditional or feudal landholdings, an advantage which could not easily be duplicated in West Germany. And even here there was some restorative action. Those men who had lost land were more likely than the average to know or find a landed widow whose husband had been lost in the slaughter.

One day at a hearing in the Ruhr, a German official, having spoken at length on the burden of the refugees on the West German economy, was being questioned by members of the commission. He was asked (it was my query) if it would not be a greater misfortune for Germany were the refugees to be sent home. He reflected and eventually agreed that great as was the disaster of their arrival, this would be worse. In the next years and with no visible effect from the work of our commission, the refugee problem in Germany dwindled to a not negligible concern for the old and those isolated in the rural areas of Schleswig-Holstein and Niedersachsen. In a few more years the word refugee ceased to be heard.

The German lesson affirmed that accommodation is a comprehensive thing. The new arrivals did not spare themselves until they had restored the living standards to which, previously, they had accommodated. Having reached that level, the great majority were, one may, I believe, assume, content.

71

The further lesson concerned their contribution to German recovery. The arrival, amidst its desolation, of millions of men and women determined to recover their previous way of life was a factor of unique power in German rehabilitation. What men of orthodox and sometimes simple mind attributed exclusively to currency reform, the Marshall Plan, the unique economic wisdom of Ludwig Erhard, must obviously be shared, in very generous measure, with this extraordinary human endowment, which so many at the time saw only as a burden.

Accommodation, as noted, is to accustomed levels of living. But accommodation is always more complete the lower the living standard, for then the grip of the equilibrium of poverty is the tightest, the pressure to accommodate as an alternative to frustrated effort the greatest. The difference – the vital and largely unexplored difference – between different poor communities lies in the number of their citizens who refuse accommodation and who seek escape from the equilibrium of poverty either within the community or by leaving it.

Once equilibrium and accommodation are recognized, the findings from the two journeys across Eastern Europe imagined in chapter 1 cease to be puzzling. People of different countries and regions have accommodated to different levels of living – different levels of poverty and affluence. The absolute levels of accommodation in any country change over time, but very slowly. Relative levels remain the same. This accommodation is a far more important determinant of living standards than resource endowment, external investment,[2] or the difference between capitalist and socialist development. And the equilibrium of poverty and the resulting more powerful accommodation explain the particularly stubborn persistence of poverty in the very poorest parts of the region.

Attention also now comes to focus on the important, perhaps over the years the principal, method by which, in this region and elsewhere, the problem of poverty has been solved and is still being solved. It is, to state the obvious, by the non-accommodating minority that a solution is urgently sought. And for many of these the best solution has been and is still to leave. This, early in the century for the Eastern Europeans, meant movement to the United States. In more recent times for Yugoslavs, it has meant going to the German Federal Republic. It is a plausible thought that the prosperity of the United States in this century and that of West Germany in the last two decades owe much to the large non-accommodating minority in Eastern Europe and the solution that it found. It is a matter of much importance to which I will return in chapter 8.

The view of poverty here offered is consistent with the Prebisch emphasis on the terms of trade, although we can now place his explanation in a more comprehensive context. This explanation, it will be recalled,[3] attributes much importance to the labor surplus that is

2. As an example, the principal emphasis oi Yugoslav efforts to equalize development as between the poor regions and the more affluent is on investment, in effect external, by the central government.

3. See pp. 25–6.

part of the equilibrium of poverty, the labor deficit that normally characterizes the advanced industrial community. The result is a price and income relationship that expels labor from the poor community and encourages its absorption in the more affluent industrial community. In keeping with this, the terms of trade are held to be persistently adverse to the poor country, although the facts in the case, as with most economic findings, have not escaped challenge.

The poor country or community must, indeed, export labor if income is to improve. But accommodation obviously acts against such emigration, which is to say it causes people to accept incomes in their own country which are far below those of the affluent industrial alternative. More important, accommodation will reduce the response to price. People who have so accommodated to poverty do not (and usually cannot) withdraw or reduce their production when prices are low. They accept whatever income comes from whatever is available for sale. The supply of products that the poor community sends to market will thus be relatively unvarying, relatively inelastic to price. Below a certain level, the response to market change becomes a casualty of the culture of poverty.

There is, however, both temptation and danger in attributing too much importance to the terms of trade as an explanation of mass poverty. That is because there is a beguiling symmetry in the notion that the poverty of the poor countries is the natural counterpart of the wealth of the rich. And it leads easily on to exploitation theories of mass poverty. The rich countries, buying at low prices from the poor, selling back at high prices, are responsible for their poverty. To recur to Lenin, workers and capitalists are astride the backs of the peasant masses of India, China, Africa, and Latin America.[4] To be able to see the poverty of the Third World as a legacy of past exploitation or a manifestation of present exploitation has become, in some measure, a test of political detachment for the scholar from the affluent world. To fail to attach major weight to such causation is to confess an apologist's purpose.

Yet what is rhetorically and politically compelling is sometimes a poor guide to practical action. The most drastic imaginable improvement in the terms of trade of primary products – a doubling in the price of agricultural products, metals, other materials – in relation to the products and services of the rich countries would not alleviate the poverty of the masses of India, Pakistan, Indonesia, Egypt, Mexico, or others similarly situated. Price is not decisive if you have little or nothing to sell. By far the greatest beneficiaries from such an improvement in the terms of trade just mentioned would, in fact, be the farmers (and other primary producers) of the United States, Canada, Australia, and Argentina, for it is they who have the great salable surplus. Similarly, the large multinational corporations, when they operate in poor lands, may well be powerful in their purchase of labor and materials, as also in the sale of their products. But the rural masses do not work for multi-

4. See Paul M. Sweezy, 'Socialism in Poor Countries', *Monthly Review*, October 1976. 'In effect . . . the European and North American proletariat, exploited though it was by its own capitalists, nevertheless joined in an uneasy alliance to share the fruits of the exploitation of the periphery' (p. 5).

national corporations. They would invariably improve their incomes if they did. Nor do they sell to them or in appreciable measure buy from them. Their poverty comes less from their adverse terms of trade than from having so little to trade.

Finally, there is light here – albeit an uncertain light – on the relation of colonialism and its residue of attitudes to poverty and economic development. Colonial rule excluded the subject peoples from political decision, reserved this to the interest or preference of the colonial power. The exclusion operated against the masses of the people and, to the extent possible, against the nonconforming minority. Against this exclusion, while colonial rule remained successful, there was no effective redress. The habits of acceptance so engendered could reasonably be expected to extend to all of life. Colonialism, so viewed, was a force for accommodation, one that in its aftermath could be expected to have enduring effects.

However, life again is not quite so neat. Colonial rule also had strong tutelary aspects which acted in many and varied ways against accommodation, as also, by example, did the colonial rulers themselves. And so, without question, did the sharpening of national consciousness and passion that, in much of the colonial world, was induced by the thrust for independence and the associated struggle and upheaval.

Would India, Pakistan, or Bangladesh be more developed had the British never come? Or Indonesia had the Dutch never been there? Or North Africa without the French? Whether in the longer light of history colonialism was a service or a disservice to accommodation and thus to the continuing equilibrium of poverty had best remain a subject for debate. But no one should dismiss as simple-minded and reactionary those who argue that, in its own time, the colonial experience was antithetical to accommodation. No less a revolutionary figure than Marx was firm in his belief that the British were a positive and progressive force in India.[5]

5. My former colleague Kenneth Arrow, now of Stanford, has drawn my attention to the concise observation on this point of Joan Robinson. 'The misery of being exploited by capitalists is nothing compared to the misery of not being exploited at all.' *Economic Philosophy* (Garden City, N.Y.: Doubleday, 1964), p. 45.

6

The Framework of Policy

A simple point must be emphasized. If public action on some social ill is in keeping with the broad current of circumstance, if it swims with that tide, it will work. If it is against or across that current, the results will be disappointing, frustrating, maybe cruel. So it is with action on mass poverty, with social effort to break the grip of the equilibrium by which it persists. If we have correctly identified the controlling circumstances in mass poverty, the remedial policy follows and will be effective. Disappointment was predictable in the past because such policy did not accord with circumstance. Instead, it made fact subordinate to the remedies that were available or convenient.

There are two broad lines of attack on poverty that are consistent with the circumstances as here identified. The first is to combat accommodation – to seek to enlarge the number of people who, resisting or refusing accommodation, are motivated to escape the equilibrium of poverty. The second is to facilitate that escape.

The two lines of action are deeply interdependent. There is no purpose in providing an escape from the equilibrium of poverty if people are not so motivated that they seek it. This is an intensely practical matter, one that has entered the subjective consciousness, I venture to think, of most people who have had serious experience with the poor rural communities that make up the poverty mass. Those so concerned have encountered the indifference or resistance of people to their own economic self-improvement that is the essence of accommodation. Since those so involved have been culturally conditioned by their own life in the affluent world where accommodation is the exception and derogatory, their reaction has remained subjective. One does not casually attribute an aberrant tendency to less fortunate people. At most, such reference is confined to privileged, discouraged or highly casual comment: 'One problem is that they are really lazy.' Not many, certainly, have seen the rational basis of this behavior – that the one thing worse than accepting the equilibrium and culture of poverty was to live in *hopeless* conflict with it.

But an attack on accommodation requires also that there be an alternative. To encourage and hold forth a promise of escape that is false commits those who are so persuaded to the cruel frustration that in the past has made accommodation the better solution.

This, too, is an intensely practical matter. All who are acquainted with the poor countries know of the frequent existence of large numbers of people, often younger men and women, who, primarily as the result of their education, no longer accept that they must be poor. Education has destroyed accommodation. Yet no alternative opportunity exists or seems to exist; escape is not possible or does not so seem. These men and women, referred to in India, Pakistan, and elsewhere as the educated unemployed, show in strong and bitter relief the danger of seeing policy on poverty in partial terms. It is entirely possible that to do so may enhance rather than reduce the anguish that is associated with poverty.

Policy to facilitate the escape from the equilibrium of poverty, accommodation being defeated, has two further and closely interdependent aspects. It can involve efforts to facilitate escape within the equilibrium of poverty, within the culture so held in bondage, and it can involve support to escape from that culture. The individual who rejects accommodation can be supported in his efforts to break out of the conventional mode of agricultural production – to acquire land, fertilizer, water, better seed, pest control and the capital required for these, and thus improve his income progressively. Or he can be helped to find alternative employment either within or outside his own country. The escape from the equilibrium of poverty, as distinct from the escape within the equilibrium, has been in modern times by far the most important recourse.

However, as noted, escape from the equilibrium and escape within it are symbiotic. The equilibrium of rural poverty owes its intractability to the relationship of people to land – to a population so numerous and dense in relation to land resources that, even when all share equally in the product, all are poor. Being poor, there is no surplus for the investment that improvement requires. This too is excluded by the sheer pressure of numbers. When land is divided among many cultivators into minuscule plots, much technical advance (machine cultivation is an obvious case) is impossible. The technical improvement which is possible – improved fertilizer use or better seed stock – is without necessary companion changes in soil and water management. And, in any case, the small scale of operations leaves the cultivators still poor, the equilibrium unbroken. The departure of the people, if in sufficient numbers, can pave the way for a reorganization of the agriculture, the breaking of the equilibrium. I have earlier adverted to the expulsion of the people from the Scottish Highlands at the end of the eighteenth and beginning of the nineteenth centuries – the famous Clearances. This paved the way for more extensive and profitable sheep husbandry and eventually broke an age-old equilibrium of poverty there. The Irish who departed Ireland at the time of the famine, and thereafter, made good their own escape from poverty and made possible the escape of those who remained behind. Until thirty years ago, the poverty of the rural South was strongly, if ineffectively, on the American conscience. Succor of one sort or another – the Resettlement Administration, later the Farmers Home Administration, improved technical services to the tenant poor – was assumed to be the answer. The answer was, in fact, a mass escape from the area – from the cotton and sharecropper equilibrium of poverty. It will be suggested that this moved the problem to the cities. However unpleasant, urban poverty is a less comprehensive and a less stable and intractable form of deprivation.

There is a decided constant in this experience. For the individual, escape from the culture of poverty has always been the most practical solution. And this escape repeatedly has made possible the breaking of the equilibrium that sustains the culture. But policy has regularly emphasized the opposite priority. Efforts to facilitate escape within the equilibrium – to improve the agricultural methods of the poor countries – have contended strongly with measures which allow of escape from agricultural poverty. Industrialization and the associated urbanization – the escape to urban employment – have not usually been thought as wholesome as remaining on the farm. The poor lands have regularly been rebuked for placing too much emphasis on industrial development and employment. Far better to invest in agriculture. In the prescription for human betterment, there is no greater constant than the belief that poor people are better off if they remain very poor but in fresh air.

Especially where this remedy has an international aspect – involves movement from poor countries to rich – it is, by tacit agreement between the rich countries and the poor, all but banned from discussion. First efforts must be devoted to finding 'attractive alternatives to migration' for people at home.[1] This is a matter for more specific attention in a chapter to come.

The attack on poverty begins, as noted, with the problem of accommodation. Some will openly urge,

1. 'Declaration of Principles and Programme ol Action adopted by the Tripartite World Conference on Employment, Income Distribution and Social Progress and the International Division of Labour', Geneva, Switzerland, 4–17 June 1976, pp. 9–11. One of the aims of this conference was to set up guidelines to protect migrant workers.

and many more will think, that it should end there. The case is part of the oral literature of the ages. People are poor but happy. Why stir them up, cause discontent?[2] They are loved by God, which is why there are so many of them. Those who subscribe to these doctrines may be more secure than they know. To counter accommodation is not easy. As a broad rule, it is possible not within generations but only between generations; once an individual has made his peace with poverty, he is unlikely again to resist. And the question is never of the accommodation or non-accommodation of a whole population. It is, to remind, a question of the number – the proportion of the population – that does or does not accommodate.

The methods by which accommodation is broken are not in doubt. They are trauma and education. In the past it has most often been by trauma – famine, military depredation, pogroms, forced expulsion of inconvenient or nonconforming ethnic or religious groups, landlords with a vision of a better use of their land. None of these measures recommends itself as civilized procedure. What remains is education. It is

2. My own resistance to these thoughts will, I trust, be evident. Paul Streeten, the distinguished British authority on these matters, has recently used language that I would readily adopt to express it: 'In my view, the most fundamental argument for [overcoming poverty] . . . is that human beings, wherever born, should be able to develop to the fullest extent their capacities, both in order to fulfil themselves and in order to contribute to the common heritage of civilization.' 'It *is* a moral issue', Oxford University Institute of Commonwealth Studies Reprint Series, no. 83E, p. 2. Reprinted from *Crucible*, July/September 1976 (London: General Synod Board for Social Responsibility), pp. 108–12.

not by itself a sufficient measure, but it is an absolutely necessary one.

It is by universal education – literacy and its employment – that individuals gain access to the world outside the culture of poverty and its controlling equilibrium. Other things also serve – the example of those who have escaped, travel, radio. (Though accommodation is not mentioned, these are regularly cited as sources of motivation.) But *only* education allows the individual to be continuously in touch with the world outside, gives him a measure of control over that access and helps him when and as he makes his escape. Travel, the example of a successful farmer, may be effectively adverse to accommodation. Their effect, however, is on a particular individual. They do not work, as does education, on an entire educable generation to select those most susceptible to escape. Nor do they have the continuing and cumulative effect that literacy allows in access to the mind. And they do not leave the individual with a useful, perhaps indispensable, instrument for escaping the equilibrium.

Repeatedly one is impressed with how effectively the untutored instinct of the last century fostered economic development – how much better on occasion it was than the much more careful and deliberate analysis of our own day. The unerring emphasis on transportation as an instrument of economic development is one example. The attention paid to free *and* compulsory education is another. Education was made compulsory because it was recognized, in effect, that nothing less would break the accommodation of the poorest families to their poverty.

That this accommodation was strong, and increasingly so with declining income, was recognized, even taken for granted, into my own lifetime. In rural Ontario a half a century ago, to recur to that obvious source of personal instruction once more, the poorest farm families, with only the rarest exceptions, most resisted the requirements of the educational authorities and the opportunities of the local school. Their offspring appeared in the autumn after farm work was over, disappeared with the frost in the spring. There was a general and often explicitly stated feeling that education was a dangerous thing – that it made the young 'dissatisfied with their lot', which was to say with perfect accuracy that it was an assault on accommodation. In most cases, this education did not, in fact, break the accommodation. But for some it did. And for the rescue of this minority, as well as for the purely practical utility of a little learning for those who did not allow education to interfere with accommodation, compulsion was rightly deemed necessary.

Much, no doubt, remains to be said about the kind of education that best defeats accommodation. This is not part of my competence. One can only assume that the more that is available and required, the larger will be the proportion of the population that will be led to resist accommodation. What is, however, certain is that basic education must always take precedence over more technical or sophisticated instruction directly related to improvement in economic performance. In recent times, large, sometimes enormous, efforts have been made to teach advanced agricultural methods to illiterate villagers. It has seemed a plausible short-cut to improved output and income. The results more often than otherwise have been disappointing and to those pursuing the effort sometimes demoralizing. The sequence was twice wrong. Education was necessary to break the accommodation. It was also very much a prerequisite to understanding and accepting the ideas underlying or justifying the technical innovations.

Given rejection of accommodation, the possibility of escape within the equilibrium of rural poverty then arises. Instruction in improved agricultural methods, together with support to the required investment, becomes feasible. Two features are essential. Such effort must follow, not precede, the general educational attack on accommodation, as just noted. And it must be directed not at all farmers but only at those for whom the effort against accommodation has been successful – those who are motivated to escape the equilibrium of poverty. Both requirements, though of the highest importance, have again been inconsistent with past practice. As noted, efforts at agricultural improvement have regularly had priority over the basic education which contends vitally with accommodation. And the normal test of such effort is the proportion of all farmers it is reaching. Nothing in the past has so criticized efforts at agricultural improvement as the charge that 'they are reaching only a small minority of producers. They are not reaching the poor farmers.' There should be no such effort to reach the indifferent farmers. Agricultural extension should reach only those who resist accommodation, who seek escape from the equilibrium of poverty. These, normally, are a minority.

Frequently they are a small minority. Any effort designed for more will contribute to its own frustration.

Practical experience bears out the importance, even binding urgency, of the rules just cited. In India in the early fifties, an ambitious village development program was initiated under the energetic leadership of S. K. Dey, minister for community planning. Steps were taken to establish a source of technical guidance and leadership for all cultivators in every substantial agricultural community in India. This village-level worker was backed by specialists in agronomy, soil and water management, and pest control and by other experts responsible for a larger area. The effort evoked the unique enthusiasm of American agricultural specialists, for it paralleled in broad outline the Cooperative Extension Service with its system of county agents in the United States. Such agricultural specialists, not without selflessness and goodwill, may be the world's greatest cultural imperialists. What exists in the United States should exist and will work anywhere else in the world. The effort also had the warmhearted and substantial support of the Ford Foundation.

The village development program was a disappointment; whatever its more limited achievements, it did not, over India as a whole, break the equilibrium of poverty. And, while the reasons given have been variously stated, all are in keeping with this analysis.

The poorly trained village-level worker could not contend with the technical inertia of the village, which is to say its accommodation to the culture of poverty.[3]

3. On this see Gunnar Myrdal, *Asian Drama: An Inquiry Into the Poverty of Nations*, abridged ed. (New York: Pantheon, 1971), pp. 177–8.

It was commonly observed that he tended to sink into the life of the village – in effect, to accommodate himself.

The effort was directed at all villages and all farmers. Such results as it had, in keeping with this analysis, were confined to the non-accommodating minority – to rewarding, in Myrdal's words, 'primarily those who are already better off than most'.[4] With the passing years, hopes for the effort declined and enthusiasm waned. A number of show villages continued to impress the more susceptible foreign visitors.[5] The accommodation to the culture of poverty remained an unbroken barrier to change.

Had the resources used for community development been employed on basic education – on countering accommodation – there would now be a larger group open to help in the escape. Such resources as were available for agricultural improvement should have been concentrated on the individuals and areas already motivated to employ them. Experience also affirms this

4. ibid., p. 178.

5. In the spring of 1961, Lyndon Johnson, then vice-president, was taken to see one of these villages in the neighborhood of Agra. It was, of the several hundred thousand villages of India, the same one that Dwight D. Eisenhower had been shown a year or two before. It was impressive in its cleanliness, simple cultural life, handicrafts, and evidence of progressive agricultural techniques. Johnson, an old hand in problems of agricultural uplift and difficult to deceive, then demanded to see the adjacent village a mile or two away. After strong protesting words about its lack of preparation to receive him, he was taken there. This village, one judged, had undergone no major technical, cultural, or hygienic change in the previous thousand years.

course. Where, as in the Punjab, the levels of literacy were high and the rejection of accommodation also fairly common, these and associated or later programs of agricultural improvement did have a substantial effect on production and income.

7

The Industrial Escape

Economic development consists in enlarging the opportunity for those so motivated to escape the equilibrium and culture of poverty. As observed earlier, this escape can be within the culture or from it. The latter can be non-agricultural employment, in practice industrial employment, within the country. Or it can involve migration to such employment in other countries. It is hard to think of a subject on which, viewing the accrued mass of writing, there would appear to be so little unsaid as on industrial development. Not much can be added or repeated here. But the basic terms of the relation of industrialization to policy on mass poverty must be outlined.

It will be evident that the instinct which sees industrialization as a vital element in the attack on mass poverty is sound. It is not alone that industrialization provides the products that go into any living standard which moves above the deprivation level. It is equally or more important an alternative to life within the equilibrium of poverty.

Repeatedly in the last thirty years, there has been complaint that economic development efforts have been negligent of agriculture, unduly committed to industry and other urban improvement. There is conflict between agriculture and urban industry, and the latter wins. 'The most important class conflict in the poor countries of the world today is not between labour and capital. Nor is it between foreign and national interests. It is between the rural classes and the urban classes. The rural sector contains most of the poverty, and most of the low-cost sources of potential advance; but the urban sector contains most of the articulateness, organization and power.'[1]

That industrialization should be given priority reflects a sound instinct. It has, in all modern economic development, been the major recourse and opportunity for those seeking escape from rural poverty. The question concerning urban industrial development is not its priority but the uncertainty as to how it is assured. The modern discussion of how industrial development is achieved in the poor country is, in fact, an intellectual curiosity of the first order; it proceeds from almost perfect certainty as to what will serve industrialization, but there is also almost total uncertainty as to the result of any given line of action. Were the means for getting

1. Michael Lipton, *Why Poor People Stay Poor: Urban Bias in World Development* (Cambridge: Harvard University Press, 1977), p. 13. This is a powerfully argued case, and part of it I would accept. Mr Lipton's case against urban investment, on 'urban motorways', 'world boxing championships in showpiece stadia', is valid, and my emphasis on general education as a prerequisite to rural development implies a heavy rural investment. In later stages of development, Mr Lipton concedes a parity, if not a priority, for industrial investment. However, we differ on the basic point, and our difference is sharpened by the skill with which Mr Lipton makes his case.

industrial development known, nearly all of the poor countries would now be on the way to industrial success. Almost all wish to be industrialized. Success would be the rule and not, as now, the exception.

It follows that the counsel that poor countries receive, for all its assurance, may not be very good. It is not.

The most serious case could be the socialist advice. Socialists can hardly avoid urging socialism, urging against free enterprise or capitalism. The consequence - reliance on a large, centrally planned and administered public sector - is that the greatest possible claim is placed on the scarcest possible resource. That is administrative talent, with its complementary requirements in expert knowledge, experience, and discipline. This is tapped in the most prodigal possible manner. The market as a governing mechanism is erratic, capable of inflicting much pain, and often morally indefensible in its distribution of income. The affluent country can temper the action of the market, even dispense with it in greater or less measure, and does. The administrative substitutes are available, even abundant. For the poor country the entrepreneur and the market are inevitable. They do not have to wait on administrative decision; they decentralize and multiply the intelligence that is brought to bear on productive activity; and, above all, they economize on scarce and honest administrative talent. Failure to recognize this - to recognize that economic policy is a choice of lesser evils - has led, in the Third World, to an impressive array of failed monuments to planned development and public enterprise.[2] Where the effort has not been aborted but, as, for example, in Burma, has persisted, the results have been very grim.

The case of China, a very poor country which is attempting a comprehensive socialist development and with much evidence of success, will be cited as proof against this case. This is doubtful. For China, of all the countries in the world, has the greatest experience in organization, administration, and acceptance of the associated discipline – it had an orderly, centralized, and successful system of public administration when the Western European polity had not proceeded beyond tribal leaders carrying clubs and wearing skins. It is quite possible, in consequence, that China is better able to meet the administrative claims of socialism than, say, the Soviet Union. That something works in China is no guide to its feasibility elsewhere in Asia or in Africa or Latin America.[3]

The advice on industrial development from the capitalist world has been marginally better than that from the socialist countries. But, paradoxically, only

2. This point is far from original with me. It was strongly made by my colleague Edward S. Mason some twenty years ago at a time when euphoria over the possibility of planned development was general. See his *Economic Planning in Underdeveloped Areas: Government and Business* (New York: Fordham University Press 1958), pp. 72–80.

3. 'Do I, after having written books and countless articles to the contrary, now think that it is possible to build socialism in a small, desperately poor African nation? No, I do not. I still think that a certain level of technology, of abundance, and a democratic sophistication among the masses, a capacity for self-government, in the

because, without intending it, it has been more faithful
to the precepts of Marx and Lenin. Marx urged with
great and persistent eloquence that economic and
political development was firmly sequential. Capitalism
was an essential prerequisite to socialism; it developed,
in modern terms, the industrial discipline and experience that made the later transition to socialism
possible. It provided, more than incidentally, something to socialize. No one would have been more
attracted than Marx to the view that, in the poor
country, administrative capacity is a scarce resource,
that this must develop before socialism can succeed.

Before his death, Lenin had also come, as a practical
matter, to agree. Before taking power, he had scoffed
at the administrative tasks of socialism, seeing them
primarily as a problem of 'accounting and control'.
After assuming power, he reverted out of necessity in
the New Economic Policy (NEP) to a substantial
measure of capitalism. The administrative tasks of
socialism were too great for the primitive (though vast)
Soviet bureaucracy. It is the singular advantage, almost
unrecognized, of non-socialist countries that they are
not impelled to urge extensive public ownership and
central planning on the poor countries.

But it has been the advice of the non-socialist world
that, if governments in the poor countries are sufficiently anti-Communist or conservative and if capital
is made available, industrial development will take
place. If the investment climate is secure and benign,

economic as well as the political structure, is necessary for socialism.'
Michael Harrington, *The Vast Majority: A Journey to the World's
Poor* (New York: Simon and Schuster, 1977), p. 195.

then even the capital will come. This is egregiously optimistic. Even an abundance of capital in an ostensibly secure environment does not ensure industrial development. This is at least partly the lesson of the OPEC countries in very recent years.

But, though a comprehensive socialist model is disastrous, effective government remains necessary. No country that has industrialized in modern times, not Japan, Taiwan, Brazil, Mexico, or Iran, has done so without intensive intervention and support by the state.[4] The basic essentials in such intervention and support are also reasonably certain: (1) There must be adequate security for people against physical threat to their property, against expropriation or predacious taxation. (2) There must be a basic and reliable system of roads, ports, electric power supply, and communications. (3) There must be a supply of capital – in practice much of it under public auspices from outside the country – for investment by private and public borrowers, and an intelligent and honest organization for receiving and passing on loans. (4) There *probably* need to be some publicly sponsored industries – pilot-fish industries that, much argument to the contrary, have the peculiar merit of bringing others in their wake. Steel, if the country is large enough, and chemicals or petrochemicals, including fertilizer production, are possible examples.

No mention is made of training and specialized education. Opportunity, especially for the latter, is necessary, and it could be added to the list. But, if all else is available, it is reasonable to expect that this will

4. A point also urged by Michael Harrington. ibid. p. 224.

be sought and obtained. Industrialization is the counterpart of release from accommodation and escape from the equilibrium of poverty. Its prime purpose is to employ those motivated to escape. The escape ensures their availability, and the motivation ensures, in the main, that they will seek to prepare themselves for the various kinds of industrial employment. If the requisite institutions for such training do not exist, they will be urged.

For the inherently weak government, what is here suggested is not minimal. It is, in fact, a great deal. If more is attempted, it is quite possible that less will be achieved. The instinct of the earlier times that for what was once called 'industrial progress' the foregoing should be done and done well remains a guide.

It would be consistent with the convention of spurious certainty that attends all discussion of economic development to say now that, if the foregoing steps are taken, the requisite industrialization will surely follow. From this will be born the self-sustaining development which will draw more people from the countryside, allow of the reorganization and increased incomes there which, among other things, will provide the market for the industrial products.

In fact, industrial development may occur, and it may not occur. As the requisites of industrialization remain uncertain, so equally uncertain but much more so is the response to a seemingly favorable context. Were it otherwise, as noted, industrialization would everywhere succeed. No country would rise, with whatever effort, to the obtuseness or ideological commitment which would make it possible to overlook an obvious and well-traveled path. But the uncertainty of response remains. Industrial development, even under favoring conditions, is highly uncertain as to both time and magnitude. Whoever introduced such uncertainty in so needful an effort is open to criticism.

It follows that although industrialization offers an escape hatch for those rejecting accommodation, it remains an unpredictable design. The temptation to socialism arises here: if the state does something, then, seemingly, it gets done. Alas, if the state is weak, this is not the case. The administrative resources of the state must still be conserved and used to provide favoring conditions – transportation, security of persons and property, communications, power, and the education that is important both for supplying improved manpower and for acting against accommodation. If the state apparatus is overstrained by planning and the creation and operation of public enterprises, then these essentials will go by the board.

So, for those escaping the equilibrium and culture of poverty, industrialization within the country can be a possibility but not a firm promise. And both time and scale of opportunity may be adverse. So, if one is talking seriously about providing such an escape, one must offer something more assured. At this point, the responsibility and also the opportunity of the rich countries become definite, precise and very great. And a remarkable though greatly unnoticed symbiosis of interest becomes evident between those individuals seeking escape from poverty and those who need their hands and effort.

8

On Migration

Over the last two centuries the individuals seeking escape from the equilibrium of poverty – rejecting accommodation – have had one remarkably certain recourse. For most of those who have attempted it, it has served well. For their children even better. It has only rarely required any active effort on the part of governments. More often it has needed only their acquiescence and, most often, in recent times, only their non-vigilance. It has placed no strain on the capacity for public action of the poor countries. Where fully exploited, it has not only involved the escape from poverty for those directly involved, but it has facilitated escape within the equilibrium of poverty for those motivated to a different course. It is a remedy for those rejecting accommodation that is now being employed on a scale greater than ever before. As a policy for poverty, it evokes relatively little discussion. Most courses on economic development are given, many books on the subject are written, without any mention of it whatever.[1]

1. A substantial volume of research and writing has recently been done on the subject in Europe, most of it, not surprisingly, on the social and economic impact of migration on the receiving

The recourse is for those who reject accommodation to move from the poor country to one of the advanced industrial nations. As a remedy for poverty, it focuses with precision on those for whom such a policy is alone workable and for whom it must be designed – those who, rejecting accommodation, are motivated to improve their economic position. No effort or money is wasted on those not yet so motivated. One marvels, on occasion, at our capacity, especially where social convenience seems to be involved, to ignore the obvious. It was never so worthy of wonder as here.

The history of the remedy is multivariate, and it is a story of general success. Mention has already been made of its use in the Scottish Highlands and in Ireland. There the movement to the United States, Canada, and England solved the problem of poverty both for those who left and for those who remained behind. The grip of the equilibrium of poverty in Scotland and Ireland was, in time, permanently relaxed.

In those countries accommodation was broken by savagely traumatic force. Such cruelty no longer being

---

countries. See Catherine Jones, *Immigration and Social Policy in Britain* (London: Tavistock Publications, 1977), and *The Role of Immigrants in the Labour Market*, Project Report by the Unit for Manpower Studies (London: Department of Employment, 1977) This latter publication includes a useful survey of recent literature from Germany and other countries on migration. The International Labour Office in Geneva has currently in progress a massive series of studies on migration but with particular emphasis on the economic development of labor-intensive industries in the countries of origin as an alternative to migration.

recommended, earlier discussion retreated to education and the awareness, discontent, and qualifications for alternative employment which it breeds and provides. But force has not always been necessary. In Eastern Europe in the last century, the pogroms were unquestionably helpful for resisting the pressure, operative over many centuries, for Jews to come to terms with the low living standards of the communities to which they had come. But Jews, by the standards of the time, were relatively well-educated and socially aware. Many moved to the United States and Britain without the immediate lash of fear. And millions of non-Jews in the Russian Empire, the Balkan states, Hungary, Romania, and Poland similarly rejected accommodation and made their escape, mainly to the United States.

All who so moved, almost without exception, bettered their own position. They also, no one now doubts, contributed enormously to the economic well-being of the United States and the other countries to which they came. From Italy, with similar benefit to themselves and the recipient countries, many millions more came to the United States, Canada, and Argentina. Had they remained at home, they would have added to the pressure of people on land and reinforced the equilibrium of poverty in the communities from which they came.

The clearest case, perhaps, is Sweden. In the last century Sweden (then in union with Norway) was one of the poorest countries in Europe. Some 90 per cent of the people lived in the countryside – in the characteristic equilibrium of poverty. After 1860, paralleling in time the development of public education but aided also in the sixties by serious food shortages and hunger, accommodation was increasingly rejected. In the half century between 1861 and 1910, more than a million Swedes moved to the United States. This and the companion escape to local industry broke the equilibrium of poverty in the Swedish countryside. Rural Sweden, once so poor, became prosperous. It would not have become so had the people remained on the Swedish farms and in the farm villages. As did the Scotch and the Irish, the Swedes who moved solved their own problem of poverty and that of those who remained at home. Initially, as in all other cases, they were regarded with grave misgiving by the earlier arrivals in the United States. Swedes were thought deficient in manners, attire, mode of living, and, most seriously, in quick intelligence. The belief that they contributed vastly to the well-being of those who had preceded them is now not only undisputed but affirmed in the ethnic and national faith. One must surely rejoice in the discovery of a remedy for poverty where no one, those involved or those affected, can, in the fullness of time, be deemed to have lost.

The solution was effective because it responded accurately to the equilibrium of poverty in Europe and the nature of accommodation. In each national and ultimate village community it singled out those who rejected accommodation. No one should think the number small; even in relation to massive modern population statistics it was substantial. In the ninety years after 1846, some 52 million people are estimated to have left Europe for other lands. In roughly the same period (1821–1932), 32 million came to the United States.[2]

The escape from Europe in the last century of those who rejected accommodation and the breaking of the equilibrium of poverty there are well written into the history of the age. They have a mildly heroic aura. What is not acknowledged is that this remedy continues to operate on a vastly greater scale than ever before.

It now takes a different form. Once when those rejecting accommodation arrived in the new country, they were there for good. They came with their families; there was no thought of return; they merged with the established population or the earlier arrivals, became citizens, voters, and eventually full participants in the society.

Now they are more likely to come alone, in many cases illegally. And, illegally or legally, they remain socially and politically in suspense. They live in a half-world over which there continues to hover the possibility or the threat of going home. In Europe they are the foreign workers; in the United States they are the illegal immigrants. They share the ancient characteristics of having found an effective escape from the equilibrium of poverty into which they were born, of contributing greatly to the well-being of the countries to which they go, and of being regarded, withal, with the greatest unease.

2. Argentina (1856–1932) got 6.4 million; Canada, 5.2 million; Brazil, 4.4 million; and Australia (1861–1932), 2.9 million. 'Migration', *Encyclopedia Britannica* (Chicago: William Benton, 1968), vol. 15, p. 423.

It is into Western Europe that the movement is most visible and highly organized. Those rejecting accommodation in rural Turkey, rural Yugoslavia, southern Italy, rural Spain and Portugal and, in slight measure, Finland move to Germany, France, Switzerland, Austria, the Low Countries or Sweden. Only Britain among the great industrial countries resists this movement; and only the greatest vigilance, aided enormously by its offshore location, restricts it there. West Indians, Indians, Pakistanis, and Bengalis came in large numbers before the gates were closed, as, for a long time, had the rural poor from Ireland. The policy against this migration is one of the historical curiosities of our time. It is enforced by conservatives, almost certainly to the damage of the British economy. And only one generation divides the Tories who defended the Empire from those who defend the home island from the erstwhile Empire. God must smile.

In Europe the numbers who have used this escape from the equilibrium of poverty are impressive. In 1974, West Germany had 2·4 million active foreign workers – Turks, Yugoslavs, Italians, Greeks, in that order of number. They comprised 9·1 per cent of the labor force. France had 1·96 million Algerian, Portuguese, Italian, Spanish, and other migrants, amounting to 9·3 per cent of the labor force. France, characteristically, was making slightly greater relative use of migrant labor than was the German Federal Republic, while celebrating the policy far less. However, in relation to size, by far the most important escape hatch was Switzerland where, in 1975, just under 24 per cent, roughly one-quarter, of the active labor force was from Italy, with much smaller contingents from Spain, Yugoslavia, and a scattering of other countries.

If one thinks, as one should, of the provision of work opportunity to those rejecting accommodation as one of the most practical and certain lines of attack on rural poverty, the Swiss lead the whole world, comparatively speaking, in effort. There is, however, no European industrial country which does not render some service. Austria, at the time indicated, relied on Yugoslavia for 7·2 per cent of its active labor force. Belgium, in 1971, got the same percentage from abroad, the largest number from rural Italy. Five and a half per cent of the Swedish labor force in 1973 came from abroad, mostly from Finland, although with increasing drafts on the ubiquitous and much-valued Yugoslavs.[3]

Nothing is more remarkable concerning this huge population movement than its myth. The workers are seen to be indispensable. The time when they will not be needed cannot be foreseen. Yet there is an elaborately cultivated illusion that the migrants are only temporarily present, will never become full members of the community, and must one day go home. In Germany their temporary status is celebrated, with unique tact, by their name - the *Gastarbeiter* or guest workers. Guests never outstay their welcome. Were

3. All data in this and the preceding paragraph are for 1974, except where indicated, and are from the *Background Papers*, vol. II: *International Strategies for Employment* of the Tripartite World Conference on Employment, Income Distribution and Social Progress and the International Division of Labour (Geneva: International Labour Office, 1976), p. 120. The proportion of foreign to total workers was probably at something approaching a peak in the years cited. Preliminary information indicates a subsequent decline in most countries.

these workers to depart, the German economy would, in fact, be in grave peril. The great Siemens plants in Berlin, among the largest in Europe, would close down. Automobile production would come to a near halt. In 1976, some four-fifths of the assembly-line workers at the huge Cologne works of Ford were Turks.[4] And life otherwise could become uncomfortable, even perilous. In Switzerland the effects would be worse. Construction work would come to a halt. Hotel guests would go unserved. Factory work, as in Germany, would suffer. And the physical peril would be great and real. In Switzerland (as in New York) the foreign workers extensively staff the hospitals and care for the sick under the supervision of the physicians. In their sudden absence the patients would be unwashed and unfed, and the bedpans would overflow.

Paradoxically, the foreign workers have helped to maintain both stable prices and the relatively full employment of native-born workers. That is because the employment of the latter can be pressed to the limit, and the foreign workers used to fill out the areas of shortage – shortage that would otherwise result in inflationary bidding for labor.

German utilization of migrant labour not only reduced wage pressures when the German economy was operating at over-full employment because firms could obtain migrant labour for full capacity utilization at the peak of the cycle without competitive bidding up of wage rates but also led to strong productivity gains during recessions when employers were

4. In the autumn of 1976, in Dusseldorf, I asked my luncheon companion, a director of German Ford, if the company could survive without the Turks. He was appalled by the thought.

able to cut their labour forces instead of hoarding them until the upswing.[5]

The use of foreign labor also renders a notable, if less than salutary, service by keeping unemployment out of sight. The unneeded and unemployed workers of Britain or the United States are in the country and counted; the unneeded of Switzerland or Germany are in southern Italy, Turkey, or Yugoslavia, safely beyond the statistics.

No one should suppose that the remedy of migration, so neatly related to the present diagnosis, is a European phenomenon. It operates in a different form, but with, one judges, equal power, in the United States. Until the Second World War, the rural dwellers of the southern states were caught in a tight equilibrium of poverty. Cotton, a highly labor-intensive crop, had brought to the farms and plantations far more people than could scrape a decent living from the land. As earlier noted, the first efforts were, characteristically, devoted to facilitating escape within the equilibrium, to helping black sharecroppers become progressive farmers on their own. The equilibrium *was* eventually broken, but by people moving away. Before the Second World War, there were 1,466,701 black farm workers in the rural labor force of the old Confederacy, all, virtually without exception, exceedingly poor. In 1970, there were 115,303. In Mississippi, the classic cotton

5. *The Role of Immigrants in the Labour Market*, p. 190. The quotation summarizes the conclusions of G. C. Schmid, 'Foreign Workers and Labour Market Flexibility', *Journal of Common Market Studies* IX (1970–71).

state with the largest concentration of rural poor, the number had declined from 279,176 to 20,452.[6] The solution for whites trapped on the small farms of the southern Appalachians was the same. So it was, on a similar scale, for the impoverished cane workers of Puerto Rico.

But the United States, like its European counterparts, is also the focus of a large international movement. Some of this is legal, not different from that of the last century. Some, as in the case of the Vietnam refugees, reflects the classic influence of trauma. A very large amount reflects the powerful dynamic that lies behind this means of escape; it overcomes the barriers erected by law.

Thus New York City has become the escape hatch for hundreds of thousands from the poverty-ridden islands of the West Indies. These people live in the metropolis in greater or less fear of being found and returned home. The Mexican Revolution and the break-up of the hacienda system left, as in Mississippi, far more people in the countryside than the land could decently support. (An end to injustice, to remind, is not necessarily or even usually an end to poverty.) Here, too, those who reject accommodation seek to move, and many to the United States. And so natural, even inevitable, is this recourse that not all the vigilance and

6. These figures were derived from U.S. Bureau of the Census, *Sixteenth Census of the United States: 1940 Population*, vol. II, *Characteristics of the Population* (Washington, D.C.: U.S. Government Printing Office, 1943) and U.S. Bureau of the Census, *Census of the Population: 1970*, vol. I, *Characteristics of the Population* (Washington, D.C.: U.S. Government Printing Office, 1973).

ingenuity of the American border patrols come even close to preventing its use.

Were all the illegals in the United States suddenly to return home, the effect on the American economy would also be little less than disastrous. A large amount of useful, if often tedious, work in New York and other northern cities would go unperformed. Fruits and vegetables in Florida, Texas, and California would go unharvested. Food prices would rise spectacularly. Mexicans wish to come to the United States; they are wanted; they add visibly to our well-being. Approximately $120 million is spent annually and ineffectively to police our borders,[7] of which approximately 75 per cent is used to keep the Mexicans out. Without them, the American economy would suffer, as the German economy would without the Turks, Yugoslavs, and Italians.

The reason for the migration, or part of it, lies in the reaction of ensuing generations of workers to physical toil and repetitive industrial employment. The sons and especially the grandsons of field hands do not harvest fruits and vegetables. And, equally, the sons and grandsons of assembly-line workers do not go onto the line.

This means that for many agricultural and repetitive industrial processes there must be newly recruited first-generation workers from the land. These workers compare pay on a California ranch or toil on a Detroit assembly line with the even drearier or more uncertain and always worse-compensated labor in the equilibrium of poverty whence they came. The new work they find better. The following generation makes no such

7. Appendix to the Budget of the United States for Fiscal Year 1979, p. 601.

comparison. It looks at the more leisured occupations that are the next step on.

The Detroit assembly lines would not have survived by relying on the sons of automobile workers; they have survived because of their new drafts from the Appalachians and the Deep South. It was this salvation and the last-mentioned recruits that turned Detroit in a generation or two from a predominantly white city to one predominantly of blacks. Similarly in other industrial processes and other American cities. And similarly in France and Germany. In recent years the British automobile industry has been deeply and continuously troubled. One of the less noticed causes is that Britain has been trying to make automobiles (though by no means exclusively) with Englishmen.

Migration, we have seen, is the oldest action against poverty. It selects those who most want help. It is good for the country to which they go; it helps to break the equilibrium of poverty in the country from which they come. What is the perversity in the human soul that causes people so to resist so obvious a good?

The resistance has two sources – perhaps three. Social disturbance and conflict have usually followed mass movement from poor countries to the rich.[8] There was such in Boston and New York after the Irish and Italians came. In the not distant past, Jewish gangsters had a certain notoriety in New York. Then – and still – the Mafia. And the same tension and disturbance have come with the recent migrants. Now, as earlier, it is

8. Catherine Jones in *Immigration and Social Policy in Britain* details these tensions as they were aroused by successive waves of migrants – Irish, Jewish, 'New Commonwealth' – into Britain.

assumed to be a permanent affliction. Few realize how quickly acculturation occurs, how soon the tension subsides. At a minimum, there is no rational matching of the gains from migration against these costs.

The second objection arises from a classical error in economic calculation – one that economists have rightly sought to combat, with slight success, for nearly a century. That is the belief that the available employment is a fixed quantity, that immigrants simply replace those who have already arrived. The economy does, of course, grow with the labor force and, as earlier noted, with increasing returns. Of this, the German economy is manifest proof; it would be far smaller, with lower per capita income, without its imported labor. Also, as earlier noted, Germany, Switzerland, and Austria have countered fluctuations in employment since the Second World War by increasing or decreasing the inflow of foreign workers. That these workers are not damaging to the employment of native workers, the German, Swiss, and Austrian unions accept. Recent efforts to restrict arbitrarily the number of foreigners in Switzerland have been powerfully resisted by the Swiss trade unions.

Finally, there is resistance of a sort from the countries from which the people go. There is pride in the ambition to take care of one's own. There is the thought that the people are leaving to face a world of discrimination by whites, exploitation by predatory capitalists. And, a valid point, it is the most strongly motivated who are lost to their native lands.[9]

9. Guilt extends, on frequent occasions, to those who have left. For many years I have been on close terms with Indians living in

These attitudes are formidable, no one can doubt. Were they less so, such an old and evident answer to the problem of poverty for those best prepared for rescue would not have been for so long so successfully ignored. It is time, nonetheless, for people who combine compassion with a certain respect for history and economic reality to look candidly at this solution.

Migration is not, needless to say, the only solution. I do not even urge it as the principal one. Mass poverty, as these chapters seek to show, is a tightly integrated phenomenon. And so, accordingly, is the remedial action. The breaking of accommodation and the provision of the several escapes – within the equilibrium and culture of poverty, to alternative urban employment, from the country – are parts of an organic whole. And the relevant help from the rich countries – for the requisite educational, agricultural and industrial investment – equally belongs. No one can say that one part is more important than any other. But, likewise, all must be on the agenda of the poor countries and the conscience of the affluent lands. No remedy for poverty can be excluded from what is an organic whole.

---

the United States. The feeling is general among them, almost universal in my experience, that they *should* go back to their mother country, share in her tasks and problems. To yield to the higher American income is unworthy. My practice is to tell Indian students that they should take the higher pay. if offered, as a measure of realistic need and remain in the United States, if that is their inclination. My advice always arouses surprise but, I have imagined, also relief. It is what most intend to do in any case.

Index

Accommodation to poverty, 54, 66; significance of, 55, 58–61, 65; religion and, 56; escape vs., 57–8, 98–104, 107; revolt vs., 63–4; significance of rejection of, 67, 111; development vs., 68, 70–71, 96, 97; and lower living standards, 72–3; and income–price relationship, 74; colonialism and, 76–7; subjective reaction to, 79, 83; education vs., 79, 83–6, 88–9, 97, 101; trauma vs., 83, 99, 107. *See also* Escape; Income; Industry; Migration

Africa, 41, 48, 93; scarcity of educated manpower in, 19; effect of colonialism in, 24–5; industrial nations or capitalism vs. poverty in, 28, 75

Agriculture: production, as Third World criterion, 25–6; and agricultural technology and improvements, 49–51, 58, 59n, 62, 80, 81, 82, 85–6, 87–9; Punjab 'green revolution' in, 68; industrialization vs., 91; and migration of farm workers, 106; and migrant labor 108

Algeria: migrant labor from, 103

Appalachia: migration from, 107, 109

Arabian peninsula: living conditions in, 15

Argentina: as agricultural producer, 75; immigrants into, 100, 102n

Arrow, Kenneth, 77n

Aspiration, *see* Motivation

Attlee, Clement, 34; quoted, 33

Australia: as agricultural producer, 26, 75; immigration into, 102n

Austria, 17; migrant labor in, 103, 104, 110

Austro-Hungarian Empire, 19

Automobile industry: German, 105; U.S., 109; British, 109

Balkan states, 100

Bangladesh, 22, 41, 48, 61, 76

Bavaria, 70

Belgium: migrant labor in, 104

Bell, Carolyn, 30n

Bengal, 103

Birth control, *see* Demographic factors

Blacks: in rural South, 106; in Detroit, 109. *See also* Ethnicity

Bohemia, 17. *See also* Czechoslovakia

Bosnia-Herzegovina, 18

Boston: social disturbance in, 109

Brazil: state support of industry in, 95; immigration into, 102n

Buck, John Lossing, 50n

Buck, Pearl, 50n

Bulgaria, 17

Bureaucracy: and poverty, 16, 20; Soviet, 94. *See also* Government

Burma, 93

Cairo, 48. *See also* Egypt

Calcutta, 22, 48. *See also* India

Canada: as agricultural producer, 26, 75; immigration into, 99, 100, 102n

Capitalism: 'exploitation' by, 16, 77n, 110; vs. socialism, 35, 73, 92; and capital investment as remedy, 40–41, 46, 94–5; as prerequisite to socialism, 94. *See also* Income

Carnegie Corporation, 30n, 31

Castro, Fidel, 64

Catholicism: and birth control, 38

Central America, 24n, 62

China: Communist, and conquest of poverty, 16, 35, 69; industrial nations or capitalism vs., 28, 75; 'loss of,' 34; land reform in, 63; and socialism, 93

Christianity: and acquiescence, 56

CIA-supported foundations, 31

Civilization and Climate (Huntington), 23

Class structure: landownership and, 61–5

Clearances, the, 81. *See also* Scotch

Climate: as poverty factor, 22–4, 38, 39, 66–7; temperature and, 23–4, 37, 66

Climate and the Energy of Nations (Markham), 23

Colombia, 22

Colonialism: as poverty factor, 24–5; and compassion for poor, 32; Spanish, and landownership, 61; as force for or against accommodation, 76–7

Communism: and conquest of poverty, 16–17, 37; and relative living standards, 17; modern impact of, 19; fear of, and U.S. policy, 33–6; in Vietnam, 35–6

Connecticut: resources vs. income in, 15–16

Conservatism: in agriculture, 59n. *See also* Agriculture

Corporations, multinational, 26, 76. *See also* Industry

Croatia, 17, 18

Cuba: Bay of Pigs, and landlordism issue, 64

Czechoslovakia, 17, 18; refugees from, 70–71

Demographic factors: natural resources, 15–16, 72, 80; latitude, 22–3; population increase, 28, 38, 52, 53, (de-

reforms in, 61, 64–5; educated unemployed in, 79–80; agricultural program in, 87–9; migrant labor from, 103; and emigrant 'guilt', 110–11n

Indians, North American, 59

Indo-China, 35

Indonesia, 41, 48, 75, 76

Industry: lack of, as poverty factor, 19; and labor surplus, 25; and multinational corporations, 25–6, 75–6; and priority of industrialization, 90–92; and requirements for industrial development, 94–6; publicly sponsored, 95; and uncertainty of development, 96–7. *See also* Labor

International Labour Office (Geneva), 99n

Iran: living conditions in, 15; state support of industry in, 95

Irish: famine and migration of, 69, 81, 99, 101; as migrant labor, 103, 109

Israel: as model of development, 15, 68–9

Italy: immigrants from, 100, 109; migrant labor from, 103–4, 106, 108

Japan: natural conditions in, 15; state support of industry in, 95

Jews: rejection of accommodation by, 100; and social disturbance, 109

Johnson, Lyndon, 88n

Jones, Catherine, 99n, 109n

Kalecki, Michal, 51n

Kaplan, Jacob J., 33n

Kennedy, John F.: quoted, 34

Kennedy, Mrs John F.: quoted, 38n

Kenya, 22

Keynes, John Maynard, 45, 46; quoted, 32 and n

Korean War, 70

Kosovo (region), 18

Kurien, C. T., 43n

Labor: -expelling vs. -absorbing economies, 25, 73–4; and employment (government and) 46 (foreign workers and) 105–6, 110; migrant, 102–6

Landlords and landlordism, 20, 37, 61–2, 83; exploitation by, 16; revolt against, 62–4; Scottish, 69; and feudal landholdings, 71. *See also* Land reform

Land reform, 61; and equilibrium of poverty, 62–5, 80–82

Latin America, 41, 48, 93; effect of colonialism in, 25; landlordism in, 62; exploitation of, 76

Latitude: as poverty factor, 22–3. *See also* Demographic factors

Lenin, V. I., 28, 75, 94; New Economic Policy of, 94

Lipton, Michael: quoted, 91n

Living standards: natural resources and, 15–16, 72, 80; in Eastern Europe, 17; in Yugoslavia, 18–19; industry and, 19, 90–91; accommodation to, 57, 71–3. *See also*

Discover more about our forthcoming books through Penguin's FREE newspaper...

Penguin Quarterly

It's packed with:

- exciting features
- author interviews
- previews & reviews
- books from your favourite films & TV series
- exclusive competitions & much, much more...

READ MORE IN PENGUIN

In every corner of the world, on every subject under the sun, Penguin represents quality and variety – the very best in publishing today.

For complete information about books available from Penguin – including Puffins, Penguin Classics and Arkana – and how to order them, write to us at the appropriate address below. Please note that for copyright reasons the selection of books varies from country to country.

In the United Kingdom: Please write to *Dept. JC, Penguin Books Ltd, FREEPOST, West Drayton, Middlesex UB7 0BR*

If you have any difficulty in obtaining a title, please send your order with the correct money, plus ten per cent for postage and packaging, to *PO Box No. 11, West Drayton, Middlesex UB7 0BR*

In the United States: Please write to *Penguin USA Inc., 375 Hudson Street, New York, NY 10014*

In Canada: Please write to *Penguin Books Canada Ltd, 10 Alcorn Avenue, Suite 300, Toronto, Ontario M4V 3B2*

In Australia: Please write to *Penguin Books Australia Ltd, 487 Maroondah Highway, Ringwood, Victoria 3134*

In New Zealand: Please write to *Penguin Books (NZ) Ltd,182–190 Wairau Road, Private Bag, Takapuna, Auckland 9*

In India: Please write to *Penguin Books India Pvt Ltd, 706 Eros Apartments, 56 Nehru Place, New Delhi 110 019*

In the Netherlands: Please write to *Penguin Books Netherlands B.V., Keizersgracht 231 NL–1016 DV Amsterdam*

In Germany: Please write to *Penguin Books Deutschland GmbH, Friedrichstrasse 10–12, W–6000 Frankfurt/Main 1*

In Spain: Please write to *Penguin Books S. A., C. San Bernardo 117–6° E–28015 Madrid*

In Italy: Please write to *Penguin Italia s.r.l., Via Felice Casati 20, I–20124 Milano*

In France: Please write to *Penguin France S. A., 17 rue Lejeune, F–31000 Toulouse*

In Japan: Please write to *Penguin Books Japan, Ishikiribashi Building, 2–5–4, Suido, Tokyo 112*

In Greece: Please write to *Penguin Hellas Ltd, Dimocritou 3, GR–106 71 Athens*

In South Africa: Please write to *Longman Penguin Southern Africa (Pty) Ltd, Private Bag X08, Bertsham 2013*

READ MORE IN PENGUIN

BUSINESS AND ECONOMICS

The Affluent Society John Kenneth Galbraith

Classical economics was born in a harsh world of mass poverty, and it has left us with a set of preoccupations hard to adapt to the realities of our own richer age. Our unfamiliar problems need a new approach, and the reception given to this famous book has shown the value of its fresh, lively ideas.

Understanding the British Economy
Peter Donaldson and John Farquhar

A comprehensive and well-signposted tour of the British economy today; a sound introduction to elements of economic theory; and a balanced account of recent policies are provided by this bestselling text.

A Question of Economics Peter Donaldson

Twenty key issues – the City, trade unions, 'free market forces' and many others – are presented clearly and fully in this major book based on a television series.

The Economics of the Common Market Dennis Swann

From the CAP to the EMS, this is an internationally recognized book on the Common Market – now substantially revised.

The Money Machine: How the City Works Philip Coggan

How are the big deals made? Which are the institutions that really matter? What causes the pound to rise or interest rates to fall? This book provides clear and concise answers to these and many other money-related questions.

Parkinson's Law C. Northcote Parkinson

'Work expands so as to fill the time available for its completion': that law underlies this 'extraordinarily funny and witty book' (Stephen Potter in the *Sunday Times*) which also makes some painfully serious points about those in business or the Civil Service.

READ MORE IN PENGUIN

POLITICS AND SOCIAL SCIENCES

Conservatism Ted Honderich

'It offers a powerful critique of the major beliefs of modern conservatism, and shows how much a rigorous philosopher can contribute to understanding the fashionable but deeply ruinous absurdities of his times' – *New Statesman & Society*

Karl Marx: Selected Writings in Sociology and Social Philosophy
Bottomore and Rubel (eds.)

'It makes available, in coherent form and lucid English, some of Marx's most important ideas. As an introduction to Marx's thought, it has very few rivals indeed' – *British Journal of Sociology*

Post-War Britain A Political History Alan Sked and Chris Cook

Major political figures from Attlee to Thatcher, the aims and achievements of governments and the changing fortunes of Britain in the period since 1945 are thoroughly scrutinized in this stimulating history.

Inside the Third World Paul Harrison

This comprehensive book brings home a wealth of facts and analysis on the often tragic realities of life for the poor people and communities of Asia, Africa and Latin America.

Medicine, Patients and the Law Margaret Brazier

'An absorbing book which, in addition to being accessible to the general reader, should prove illuminating for practitioners – both medical and legal – and an ideal accompaniment to student courses on law and medicine' – *New Law Journal*

Bread and Circuses Paul Veyne

'Warming oneself at the fire of M. Veyne's intelligence is such a joy that any irritation at one's prejudice and ignorance being revealed and exposed vanishes with his winning ways ... *Bread and Circuses* is M. Veyne's way of explaining the philosophy of the Roman Empire, which was the most successful form of government known to mankind' – *Literary Review*

BY THE SAME AUTHOR

A History of Economics

Economics as practised is obsessively concerned with the future, yet economic ideas are very much a product of their time and place. If we are to understand modern economics, we can do so only through an understanding of its past, including the powerful and vested interests that moulded the theories to their financial advantage. This is the message of John Kenneth Galbraith's brilliant account of the history of economics.

'This book has all of his good qualities. It is well written, and almost compulsively readable. It is packed with witty remarks together with a large number of facts that are new to me. He brings the authors who interest him to life, and is especially good at demonstrating why certain problems they addressed themselves to were (and are) so important' – *The Times Educational Supplement*

with Nicole Salinger:

Almost Everyone's Guide to Economics

'Economics preempts the headlines. It bears on everyone's life, anxieties and, if more rarely, satisfactions.'

Believing that 'the state of economics in general, and the reasons for its present failure in particular, might be put in simple accurate language that almost everyone could understand and that a perverse few might conceivably enjoy', Professor Galbraith has collaborated with Nicole Salinger in an entertaining dialogue.

She leads him through a step-by-step explanation of economic ideas with such clarity that all can understand the basic nature of classical, neo-classical and Marxian economics, the role of money and banking, the *modus operandi* of fiscal monetary policy, the part played by multinationals, the reasons for simultaneous inflation and unemployment and the causes of the present crisis in international economic and monetary affairs.

BY THE SAME AUTHOR

The Affluent Society

Wittily, gracefully, devastatingly, Professor Galbraith attacks our most cherished economic myths. Why worship work and productivity if many of the goods we produce are superfluous – artificial 'needs' created by high-pressure advertising? Why grudge expenditure on vital public works while ignoring waste and extravagance in the private sector of the economy? Classical economics was born in a harsh world of mass poverty, and it has left us with a set of preconceptions hard to adapt to the realities of our own richer age. And so, too often, 'the bland lead the bland'. Our unfamiliar problems need a new approach, and the reception given to this already famous book has shown the value of its fresh, lively ideas.

'He shows himself a truly sensitive and civilized man, whose ideas are grounded in the common culture of the two continents, and may serve as a link between them; his book is of foremost importance for them both' – *The Times Literary Supplement*

BY THE SAME AUTHOR

The Great Crash 1929

'An intriguing study, Professor Galbraith has marshalled and presented his material well ... assuredly worthwhile' – *Sunday Times*

'One of the most engrossing books I have ever read' – *Daily Telegraph*

The New Industrial State

'His critique is as least as ambitious in scope, as appealing in its simplicity and as alarming in its implications as Marx's ever was. In marked contrast to *Das Kapital*, *The New Industrial State* is highly readable' – *The Times*

Money: Whence It Came, Where It Went

'Once again Professor Galbraith has written something noteworthy, and written it elegantly' – Woodrow Wyatt in the *Sunday Times*

'I can think of no single book on this subject that would give so immediate and so penetrating an insight into a subject which is not only naturally difficult, but which has also been unnecessarily complicated by the "experts"' – Eric Roll in *The Times Literary Supplement*

forthcoming:

The Culture of Contentment